POOR STUDENTS, RICHER TEACHING

MINDSETS THAT RAISE STUDENT ACHIEVEMENT

ERIC JENSEN

Solution Tree | Press

a division of

Solution Tree

555 North Morton Street
Bloomington, IN 47404
800.733.6786 (toll free) / 812.336.7700
FAX: 812.336.7790
email: info@SolutionTree.com
SolutionTree.com

Visit **go.SolutionTree.com/instruction** to download the free reproducibles in this book.

Printed in the United States of America

20 19 18 17 16   1 2 3 4 5

Library of Congress Cataloging-in-Publication Data

Names: Jensen, Eric, 1950 author.

Title: Poor students, richer teaching : mindsets that raise student
   achievement / Eric Jensen.

Description: Bloomington, IN : Solution Tree Press, [2016] | Includes
   bibliographical references and index.

Identifiers: LCCN 2016026186 | ISBN 9781942496519 (perfect bound)

Subjects: LCSH: Children with social disabilities--Education--United States.
   | Poor children--Education--United States. | Academic achievement--United
   States.

Classification: LCC LC4091 .J4576 2016 | DDC 371.826/94--dc23 LC record available at https://lccn.loc.
gov/2016026186

Solution Tree
Jeffrey C. Jones, CEO
Edmund M. Ackerman, President

Solution Tree Press
President: Douglas M. Rife
Editorial Director: Tonya Maddox Cupp
Managing Production Editor: Caroline Weiss
Senior Editor: Amy Rubenstein
Copy Chief: Sarah Payne-Mills
Copy Editor: Miranda Addonizio
Proofreader: Elisabeth Abrams
Text and Cover Designer: Abigail Bowen
Editorial Assistant: Jessi Finn

Acknowledgments

I am indebted to many but most importantly my wife, Diane. I am also enormously grateful for the saintly patience of Douglas Rife and the passion and expertise of Copy Chief Sarah Payne-Mills. Kudos to my colleague LeAnn Nickelsen, who also gave me fabulous help. I also appreciate the cover-design responsiveness of Rian Anderson. Finally, this book is dedicated to all U.S. teachers who work with high-poverty students with passion, courage, and a commitment to help them graduate college or career ready. Props to you pros; you make an irreplaceable difference for all of us!

Solution Tree Press would like to thank the following reviewers.

Jeff Dillon
Superintendent and Elementary
    Principal
Wilder School District
Wilder, Idaho

Kristine Humer
Reading Resource
Mark Sheridan Math and Science
    Academy
Chicago, Illinois

Susan Kessler
Executive Principal
Hunters Lane High School
Nashville, Tennessee

Samuel Lehman
Fifth-Grade Teacher
Terence C. Reilly School No. 7
Elizabeth, New Jersey

Carol Null
Kindergarten Teacher
Pemetic Elementary School
Southwest Harbor, Maine

Visit **go.SolutionTree.com/instruction** to download
the free reproducibles in this book.

Table of Contents

PART ONE

PART TWO

PART THREE

WHY THE GRADUATION MINDSET? 121

About the Author

Eric Jensen, PhD, is a former secondary teacher from San Diego, California. Since the early 1990s, he has synthesized brain research and developed practical applications for educators. Jensen is a member of the invitation-only Society for Neuroscience and the President's Club at Salk Institute for Biological Studies. He cofounded SuperCamp, the first and largest brain-compatible academic enrichment program, held in sixteen countries with over sixty-five thousand graduates.

Jensen has authored over thirty books, including *Teaching With Poverty in Mind, Tools for Engagement, Engaging Students With Poverty in Mind, Turnaround Tools for the Teenage Brain, Bringing the Common Core to Life in K–8 Classrooms,* and *Different Brains, Different Learners.*

To learn more about Eric Jensen's in-depth teacher workshops and leadership events, visit Jensen Learning (www.jensenlearning.com).

Preface

This book is about mindsets. How do I qualify to write a book about mindsets and poverty? I did my dissertation on poverty. I have worked successfully with over two hundred Title I schools in the United States. But there is something else you should know about me. This journey actually began in my early childhood. That's when I learned firsthand about adversity and mindsets.

My mother walked out on my two sisters and me when I was two. My dad struggled to raise three children. My first stepmother (of three total) entered my life when I was six. She was violent, alcoholic, and abusive. She made my home life a living nightmare for nine years (from ages six through fifteen). She threatened me daily, and I became a survivor who focused on dodging continual abuse through hiding, staying away from the house, living with relatives, and eating dog food for snacks. And that's the G-rated version. The viewpoint I learned from my father was, "Stop complaining, and focus on what's important." For me, that meant *survival*.

Most adults around me were dysfunctional, and my best friends also had abusive parents. Within weeks of my father's second marriage, my oldest sister moved out to live with the neighbors. My other sister moved out of the house and lived in the garage for nine years. When things got too dangerous, my father moved my sister and me away. We lived with my grandmother for a few months (I went to a new school) and my aunt and uncle (another school), and then we lived on our own (another school). My stepmother would "promise to be good," and each time we returned home, the violence would start up, and we would move out again. I went to nine schools and had 153 teachers. I was truant often and arrested twice. My daily mentality while sitting in the back of a classroom was about safety; I was asking myself, "What will it be like when I go home today?"

Why am I telling you this? First, I know what it's like to grow up in a toxic environment. I have had a loaded, cocked gun held to my head and heard, "Do what I tell you, or I *will* shoot." I acted out in class and got in trouble often. My K–12 grades were terrible, and I finished high school with a C+ average. The odds of me succeeding in life at that stage were not good. Second, this book is personal for me, and I am hoping to make it personal for you. You must understand the mindsets of those who grow up with adversity and, more important, learn the new mindsets to help your students succeed.

The next time you have a student in your class who acts out, who is frustrated by how your class is going, remember: I was one of those students, and I took it personally when a teacher did not help me succeed. When my teachers did not help me, I just stopped putting in the effort. You see, I was in school mostly because it was the law and my friends were there. But my teachers *chose* to teach. They *chose* to be at my school. They *chose* the subject and grade levels. On top of that, they were being paid to help me graduate. The choices you make do matter a great deal. These choices come from a teaching mindset, and that's what this book is about.

On the flip side, when teachers cared about and helped me, I worked hard and had a good attitude. While my own K–12 experience was not good overall, a few good teachers gave me hope, and slowly, I began to turn my life around. Their mindsets were different. I felt the impact of relationships and good teaching. Your students need you because your teaching really does matter more than you think it does. I know you are likely to be underpaid, underappreciated, and undersupported. But you still have to make choices every day of your life. So, will you help students graduate?

I realized early in life, even with a gun at my head, that I had a choice. And you do too. You always have a choice. You can choose to get better at your daily work practices, you can make smart decisions, and you can build your skill sets and help students graduate. Or you can realize this is not your fight and give up. Some staff may have already given up, even though they come to work each day. That's a loss for both the teacher and students.

If you don't know how to do your job well, it can be painfully hard. But in this book, I'll introduce new mindsets and show you how to teach differently. You'll start loving your job again. By the way, I'm not telling you the path of changing mindsets is easy; I'm telling you that it can be done, it's worth doing, and you can do it. I promise this resource will be part of your success. Let's get started!

Introduction

The title of this book, *Poor Students, Richer Teaching*, suggests a rich and poor dichotomy. But it is also about something that many poor students are not getting: *richer* teaching. Here, the word *richer* means full, bountiful, and better than ever. Teachers can make a difference in students' lives with richer teaching. They can ensure all students, regardless of background, graduate college and career ready.

All of us have narratives in our head about teaching. In this book, I invite you to think of your work as richer and abundant. Teachers who struggle with poor students might have mentalities that reinforce scarcity, blame, and negativity. At school, there are poor narratives that educators circulate, often in subtle ways, sometimes throwing them in with a true statement. For example, a teacher may say, "Last year, I just couldn't make any progress with Jason. You know, *those students* just don't get any parental support, so *what can I do*?" Notice how the teacher ends with a story about why he couldn't make progress. In this book, you will discover the rich strategies that high-performing teachers use to defeat these narratives and help students succeed.

Year after year, your K–12 Title I school culture either reinforces hopelessness and assumptions that the deck is simply stacked against you or it fosters optimistic possibilities and successes with uplifting narratives. I could fill this book with stories of real high-poverty schools that are succeeding, as I have done in other books. Yet, how many schools would you need to read about before you say, "OK, that's enough. I believe it"? I hope reading this book helps to reframe any negative narratives you struggle to carry.

About This Book

In a moment, you'll dive into the first chapter. But first I will give you an overview of the resource in your hands. Books for educators typically just tell teachers what to do. This one is different because in chapter 1, I explain *why* the suggestions in this book are relevant, important, and most of all, *urgent*. Chapter 1 is about the *new normal* in the United States, making it the *why* of this whole process. Once you finish chapter 1, my guess is that you'll be on board for the rest of the book.

Then, the book moves forward into its major theme—developing the powerful tool for change: mindset. A mindset is a way of thinking about something. As Stanford University psychologist Carol Dweck (2008) explains, people (broadly) think about intelligence in two ways: (1) either you have it or you don't, or (2) you can grow and change. In the areas of intelligence and competency, you may have more of a fixed mindset (stuck in place) or a growth mindset (capable of changing). Those with a fixed mindset believe intelligence and competency are a rigid unchangeable quality. Those with a growth mindset believe that intelligence and competency can develop over time as the brain changes and grows.

This book broadens and deepens the mindset theme to many new areas of student and teacher behaviors that you'll find highly relevant. The book continues in three parts, each highlighting a mindset.

Part one covers the positivity mindset. In chapters 2 through 7, you'll home in on your students' emotions and attitudes. Each chapter focuses on building your own rock-solid attitude of academic optimism in both your students and yourself. If you've ever put a mental limitation on any student (don't worry, we all have), these chapters are must-reads. You'll also see that brains can change, and you'll learn why positivity is so critical to your job. You'll learn the science behind hope, optimism, and gratitude. Without these life skills, you'll start losing students as they give less and less effort and sometimes even drop out. Your new, rock-solid positivity mindset will help your students soar.

Part two introduces the enrichment mindset. Chapters 8 through 13 focus on building breakthrough cognitive capacity in students. You'll see the clear, scientific evidence that shows, without a molecule of doubt, that change is possible. A big problem for students from poverty is their mental bandwidth, often known as cognitive load. Your students need a way to run their own brains better or this cognitive load makes them more likely to misbehave and struggle academically. Many students never get the skills of capacity building, but you can ensure yours build memory, thinking skills, vocabulary, and study skills.

Part three includes the graduation mindset. Chapters 14 through 17 help you focus on the gold medal in teaching: students who graduate job or college ready. Each chapter centers on school factors absolutely proven to support graduation. You'll learn the science of *why* these factors can be such powerful achievement boosters. Plus you'll discover a wide range of positive alternatives to what your students are doing at school.

Appendix A will help you put the implementation pieces in place. You get lesson-planning tools that show you how to design lessons with poverty in mind. Fostering the graduation mindset is the ultimate goal of this process. Appendix B offers some tips on the important process of running your own brain.

This book accompanies *Poor Students, Rich Teaching*, which covers four other mindsets to help students succeed. I have written four books on poverty, and there is still much more transformative and practical information for me to share. The topic is *that* wide and deep. As you dive in to the upcoming pages, remember this: any resource on helping students from poverty will elicit a wide range of responses.

As you read this book, it will be up to you to pause and reflect often. Any single chapter can make a difference in your work. Ask yourself not, "Have I heard of this before?" but instead, "Do I already do this as a daily practice?" and "Do I do this well enough to get the results I want or need?" The fact is that all of us can get better. This book can take you down that path. Are you game?

CHAPTER 1

THE NEW NORMAL

You have seen many changes in the United States in your lifetime. In this chapter, you'll discover the *new normal*. We typically say something is normal meaning it's *just fine* and pay less attention because we often take it for granted. We also say things are normal as if that is a good thing. But now I invite you to see the new normal as a threat to your job and your future. Poverty and mindsets (the topics of this book) play a big part of this new normal. No, this is no doomsday scenario. It is about what has *already* happened. You must know about this before you walk into your classroom again.

Hard Evidence of the New Normal

The economic changes are deepening and widening at an accelerating rate. Poverty in the United States is getting worse, not better. The new normal is this: we now have a majority of students in public schools who qualify as poor based on school data (Suitts, 2015). In the five most populated states (California, Texas, Florida, Illinois, and New York), 48 percent *or more* of public school students are in poverty (Suitts, 2015). Pause and wrap your head around this.

But it gets worse. In 2009, in the fifty largest urban school districts in the United States, the average four-year graduation rate was a jaw-dropping 53 percent (Swanson, 2009). This new normal is a mindset game changer for everyone, especially educators. The trend is not our friend.

Also part of the new normal is the disappearing middle class. Gone are many good-paying jobs that required a high school diploma and hard work (manufacturing, mining, automobiles, oil and gas, and more). Technology (robots, automated websites, and smartphones) has replaced people for many of those jobs. Trucking is the most popular job in twenty-nine states (Bui, 2015). But Mercedes has successfully tested driverless eighteen-wheelers; those trucking jobs may be eliminated soon too. Imagine that: the number-one job in over half the states will be automated (Bui, 2015).

Often poverty occurs when the cost-of-living increase does not keep pace with inflation and real wages for the middle class and poor go down. Real middle-class annual wages (adjusted for inflation) have declined dramatically, from $57,000 a year in 2000 to just under $52,000 in 2014 (Economic Policy Institute, 2014). That means the average U.S. household has lost nearly 10 percent in wages to inflation since 2000. Even for the declining middle class, life has gotten harder.

Inflation consumes any increases to the consumer paycheck as the purchasing power of the dollar diminishes. The U.S. government continually changes the measuring index for inflation by adjusting the consumer price index. Using the government's original measures from 1986, inflation averages 9 percent annually (ShadowStats.com, 2016). Has your paycheck gone up 7 to 13 percent *every* single year? If not, no wonder you feel poor.

This is the new normal, and you're not alone. Roughly 76 percent of Americans are living paycheck to paycheck, with essentially zero savings (Bankrate, 2012). The number of people on food stamps has doubled between 2008 and 2014 (U.S. Department of Agriculture, Food and Nutrition Service, 2016). About half of all children born in 2015 will be on food stamps at some point in their lives (Rank & Hirschl, 2015).

Over half (51 percent) of all American workers make less than $30,000 a year. The federal poverty level for a family of five is $28,410, and yet almost 40 percent of all American workers do not even bring in $20,000 a year (Social Security Online, 2016). See figure 1.1 for a breakdown of the new normal workforce.

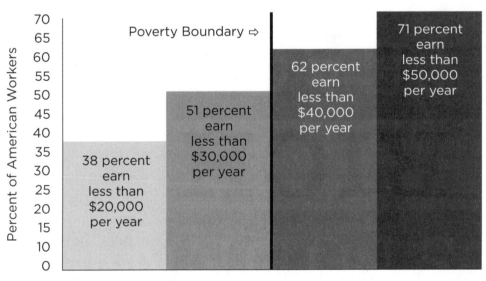

Source: Social Security Online, 2016.

Figure 1.1: The new normal workforce in America.

Let me summarize this for you. From 2000 to 2014, the share of adults living in middle-income households fell in 203 of the 229 U.S. metropolitan areas. Think about that; in almost 90 percent of the United States' metro areas, the middle class is shrinking (Pew Research Center, 2016).

Fifty-seven cities and municipalities have filed for bankruptcy since 2010 (Governing, 2015). The United States has borrowed too much, and we already owe more than we can ever repay. The government is unlikely to fix it itself; there is no precedent in world history of any country ever climbing out of debt as deep as ours. Poverty is here to stay, and it is getting worse. Wrap your head around this new normal. This is not temporary; all U.S. residents are at risk.

What More Poverty Means to You

Working with students from poverty means you'll need to deeply understand what is going on around you. Every day at work, fresh empathy is a good place to start. Then, you can improve your teaching with better mindsets and strategies. The effects of poverty on any human being are truly staggering. This book is all about how you can mitigate the adversity that students face and enrich them.

In short, poor students are different because their brains are different. The brain's neurons are designed by nature to *reflect* their environment, not to automatically rise above it. Chronic exposure to poverty affects the areas of the brain responsible for memory, impulse regulation, visuospatial actions, language, cognitive capacity, and conflict (Noble, Norman, & Farah, 2005).

Evidence suggests the brains of children from poverty are more likely to differ via four primary types of experiences: (1) health issues from poor diet and exposure to toxins and pollutants, (2) chronic stress, (3) weaker cognitive skills, and (4) impaired socioemotional relationships (Evans & Kantrowitz, 2002). While not every single child from a household with a low socioeconomic status will experience all of these factors, the majority will.

This means that you'll see behaviors that show the effects of toxins (poor memory and distractibility) or chronic stress (learned helplessness, apathy, hypervigilance, and in-your-face aggressiveness). In a classroom, you'll also see the results of less exposure to cognitive skills (deficient vocabulary, poor reading skills, and weak working memory) and impaired socioemotional skills (poor manners, misbehaviors, or emotional overreactions). Teachers who do not know what these behaviors really are may inappropriately judge a student as lazy, unwilling to follow directions, a poor listener, low achieving, and antisocial. This may foster classroom friction, a huge achievement gap, annoyed students, and even dropouts. And worse yet, the teacher may blame the behavior on the student.

You may know someone who has the impression that people don't change. In other words, some people spread lies like, "A student who is a troublemaker at age eight will always be one." This is an example of a toxic mindset. The fact is, humans can and do change. When they don't change, it is often because others have given up on them, their daily environment is toxic, or others are using an ineffective strategy that doesn't help. Every single staff member at your school should know that the human brain is designed to change if you give it a chance.

What the New Normal Means to You

I shared with you some economic facts of the new normal not to depress you but to provide an opportunity for you to develop a different understanding of poverty. It is no longer a micro problem for the poor, nor is it an outlier or something to ignore. If concerns about the United States, your paycheck, or your retirement, and the love of your students, do not motivate you to make changes, you are in the wrong profession. Poverty is the new normal in America. Only the most effective mindsets will help you succeed.

This is a sobering new reality. It is not a doomsday scenario or pessimist's dire prophecy; it already happened. This altered reality requires us to be smarter and more agile. More of the same will no longer work. Now, how does poverty connect with mindsets?

As an educator who works with schools all over the United States, I've heard just about every story there is about why students supposedly can't succeed. In rural Kentucky, I hear about coal mine closings that influence student career hopelessness. In New Mexico, I hear about how immigration fosters low expectations in students. In Hawaii, I hear about the beach culture that supposedly makes students more interested in surfing than learning. These are the devastating community-driven narratives that are killing the chances for student success.

Do you see the pattern? The stories at your school that are told and retold shape students' expectations. When the stories are upbeat, affirming, and hopeful, the students and staff reinforce a positive message. In successful schools, staff members try to redefine their new normal. Mindsets matter a great deal, especially when addressing poverty. This book will help you identify the useful and powerful mindsets that can accelerate positive change to alter the future for your students.

There is one last thing before we jump into the strategies.

In most sports, the team that scores the most points (or goals, runs, and so on) wins. This scoring system is simple and easily understood. In our profession, the scoring system that decides a winning classroom strategy is called the *effect size*. This number is simply a standardized measure of the relative size of the gain (or loss) in student achievement caused by an intervention (versus a control) (Olejnik & Algina, 2000). See figure 1.2.

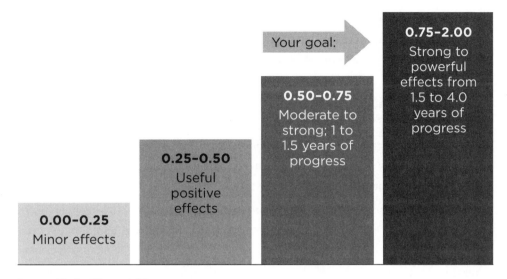

Source: *Vacha-Haase & Thompson, 2004.*

Figure 1.2: Effect sizes made practical.

Researchers simply measure the difference between doing something and doing nothing. Ideally, one uses an experimental group (using a new strategy) and a control group (using an existing norm). The strongest analysis includes large sample sizes and multiple studies with varied population demographics. Then, you know your data are very, very solid. This is important to you, so please lean in and read closely.

This is all about your teaching.

Effect sizes are a common research-based way to measure the impact of a strategy or factor. While any intervention could have a negative effect size, most classroom interventions (teacher strategies) are positive. Classroom interventions typically have effect sizes between 0.25 and 0.75 with a mean of about 0.40 (Hattie, 2009). One full year's worth of academic gains has a 0.50 effect size, and two years' worth of gains have a 1.00 effect size. This means that effect sizes above 0.50 are just the baseline for students in poverty. Teachers have to help students catch up from starting school one to three years behind their classmates. It takes good instructional practices for effect sizes to be well above 0.50.

Why do you need to know this?

What if, by just replacing one strategy you already use (for example, saying "Good job!" to a student) with another (a far more effective one, like "Your studying really paid off. Great job building your skills!"), you could get five to ten times the positive effect on student achievement? I will show you how to do that in this book. Think about the impact you can have every single workday by switching out less effective strategies with more effective strategies. In fact, I'm going to invite you to slowly replace those things you do that are *sort of* effective with strategies that are *ridiculously* effective. Yes, I am on a mission to help you become so effective that it changes the course of history for your students. But before we get started, let's summarize.

Quick Consolidation

The new normal is here. Poverty is increasing; it is not a temporary downtick in the U.S. economy. Things are getting worse, not better. The new normal means you'll be seeing more and more students from poverty. It also means that we'll collectively have to boost graduation rates of those from poverty.

When students don't graduate, they are more likely to end up in the juvenile justice track, require food benefits, or become unemployed. This, again, is no prediction; it is already happening. This book is a wakeup call. New mindsets are essential to success.

Yes, I can guarantee that the future will be bumpy, tough to predict, and unsettling. Something will likely replace the curriculum standards again (and again). We will probably see continued political, economic, and local educational pressures. But if you're ready, it'll be a bit easier to manage. Plus, you'll be someone who thrives while others are just trying to survive. Welcome to the world of richer teaching. Let's get started.

PART ONE

WHY THE POSITIVITY MINDSET?

CHAPTER 2

SECRETS OF THE POSITIVITY MINDSET

Here you and I begin with a crucial way to think of your job: the positivity mindset. Students from poverty often come from homes where positivity is rare (Hart & Risley, 1995). But you have got to be the daily source of a student's "mental vitamins."

You may have heard teachers' comments about how students from low-income families are harder to teach or have behavior problems. (You may have uttered—or perhaps just thought—them yourself.) When working with students from poverty, it's important to understand that other factors influence their behavior. The most important trait you can sharpen is your empathy, not sympathy. Those with empathy feel others' pain. Alternatively, those with sympathy feel sorry for others. To become both positive and empathic, you've got to understand what's *really* going on. This chapter will provide that insight for you.

Student behaviors, as you may predict, often start at home. Higher rates of acute stress and trauma are more common in families from poverty. You need to know this because many students' behaviors that may be disruptive (or even offensive) may be a result of things at home that are completely out of a student's control. Persons in poor households have more than double the rate of violent victimization than those in high-income households (Harrell, Langton, Berzofsky, Couzens, & Smiley-McDonald, 2014). Additionally, a poor mother's history affects students' behaviors in your classrooms. For example, poor African American women report high rates of rape—far more than Caucasians, Latinos, and Asians. This sexual assault, in turn, causes adverse mental health effects, such as depression, guilt, post-traumatic stress disorder, suicidal thoughts, and avoidance (Ullman, Townsend, Filipas, & Starzynski, 2007). When moms have been traumatized, every day is a struggle to try to remain loving, calm, grateful, and caring. Their children often come to school with chronic stress. You have to be different and teach differently.

For immigrants, the trauma can come from the stressors and adversity that emerged from a dangerous border crossing, detention, and deportation threats. Now, you can add the problems of undocumented citizenship status, separation from family, and of course, extreme poverty. Immigrants report trauma from fear, depression, loneliness, sadness, and chronic stress (Crocker, 2015). If you don't address these issues with positive self-regulation strategies in your classroom, students can feel overwhelmed and their classroom behaviors will be seemingly crazy. And students are unlikely to graduate career or college ready.

For your students, it is just how it is. Actually, it would likely be a shock if most students from poverty came to school with any sense of hope and optimism. Instead, many teachers, some of whom are ignorant about a student's history, blame bad attitudes on the student. Students didn't choose their DNA, parents, neighborhood, or culture. Begin your day with empathy. Yes, you can change student attitudes, but you have to start by caring.

There's another source of stress for your students: racism. When your students of color feel society's bias against them, judgment from their teachers, or exclusion from the middle-class and upper-class world, it commonly generates chronic stress (Kim, Neuendorf, Bianco, & Evans, 2015). In addition, when students of color live on a constant survival track and often feel forced to respond to everyday discrimination with anticipatory vigilance, there's a cost to their health and sanity (Himmelstein, Young, Sanchez, & Jackson, 2015). This stress and anxiety change classroom behaviors and learning.

The Positivity Mindset

Developing a positive mindset in your students makes a huge difference, and in your classroom, it will alter lives. Before we understand the thinking of teachers with a positive mindset, let's contrast it with the opposite mindset. A teacher who struggles with positivity may say one or more of the following comments. Ask yourself if you have occasionally heard these comments at school.

- "Of course I try to be positive, but realistically, look at what I'm up against. Have you seen our students? Do you know where they live, their friends, and their parents? How are we supposed to succeed with them?"

- "Positivity is for the deluded. I'm real with my students. I tell it like it is. Their lives are not positive, so there's no sugarcoating to be done."

- "Listen, our administration doesn't even care, so why should I be positive?"

- "I'm a pretty positive person. It's just that those lazy delinquent students don't want to learn, and our blood-sucking administrators and district morons take all the fun out of our job. I mean, really, the pay sucks, and they treat us like criminals half of the time. But mostly I still try to be positive."

When the comments are written down, they seem mind boggling, don't they? As you reflect on comments such as these, consider your own mindset. Put yourself in a parent's shoes. Now, if your own son or daughter had teachers making these comments, how would you feel?

I hit rock bottom several times in life. I bet maybe you have too. I remember being so desperate, I was writing bad checks weekly just to survive. I could no longer afford housing, and I was going bankrupt. I had no one to turn to except my cynical business partner. We became drinking buddies and soon, we both got worse. I'm telling you this not because I want sympathy nor am I assigning blame. At that time in my life, I really needed genuine hope. I have been asked many times, "What turned you around?"

I have discovered that sometimes to find myself, I had to see what the opposite of me was like. When I was thirty, I met some amazing positive role models. For the first time in my life, I saw possibility and regained hope that I could become someone different and better. But I could not have told you that I needed them (nor will your students articulate that they need you). As you might guess, that's not the mindset we want. The positivity mindset says, "I am an optimistic and grateful ally who helps students build a successful narrative of their future."

The positivity mindset says, "I am an optimistic and grateful ally who helps students build a successful narrative of their future."

In contrast with the teachers' negative comments, there are many other teachers with a positive mindset who I have heard make comments like the following.

- "Teaching is my life's mission; I love to help students succeed. The satisfaction I get is priceless."

- "I love my job. Of course, it's not perfect, but life is what you make it. I choose my positive energy every day because that's what my students need."

- "I choose to be optimistic because it feeds me and feeds my students. My job is to supply the hope and faith that they can make it in this world."

- "I can't control what happens to me in life, but I can control my thoughts and my responses to life. Knowing I have that control helps make my students and me happy."

Do those comments sound like the teachers are a bit crazy, or have they found a way to feel at peace, do good things, and still be pretty happy most of the time? In short, is there any real proof that either point of view is any better than the other? Can we say that these viewpoints, although very different, don't really matter to the students? Let's look at the evidence.

A Hard Look at the Evidence

Now, before you respond with an opinion about this mindset (it may sound a bit delusional or new age), let's look closely at the scientific and biological evidence of whether this mindset is valid in your classroom.

The Impact of Positivity on Student Success

Researchers placed microphones in the homes of upper-class, middle-class, and lower-class families (with permission, of course) for two months in order to measure positive and negative remarks (Hart & Risley, 1995). When they analyzed the audio recordings, researchers found that, among the poor, the ratio was 1:2 (one positive for every two negatives—reprimands, criticisms, and so on). In middle-class homes, the ratio of positives to negatives was the reverse: two positives for every one negative. How did the upper-class families do? They heard six times more positives than negatives (Hart & Risley, 1995, 2003). Figure 2.1 illustrates this disparity.

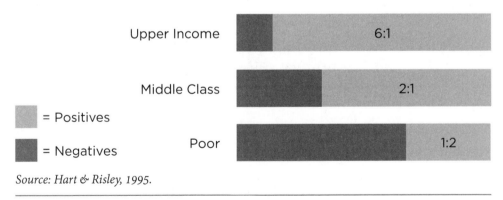

Source: Hart & Risley, 1995.

Figure 2.1: The effects of socioeconomic status on positive to negative comments.

This study shows that income level does correlate with household differences in emotional positivity. Students from poverty do not need negativity from peers, parents, or teachers. They need a positive environment every day. If you want students from poverty to behave, learn, and grow like well-behaved people, treat them better. You want to make your classroom the best place to learn on earth.

Do students' feelings predict success? Studies show positive emotions influence cognitive flexibility and perseverance, both powerful traits in those who achieve academically (Liu & Wang, 2014). The poor, however, more commonly feel hopeless or overwhelmed (Behnke, Piercy, & Diversi, 2004; Honora, 2002). This means that in your classroom a positive mindset is essential for you to have. Your students must learn to see their world better if they're going to succeed.

Why should you care about fostering a positive classroom climate? Studies show that induced positive emotions widen attention (Rowe, Hirsh, & Anderson, 2007). When we are upset, we narrow our attention and focus on the bad. Positive emotions increase and broaden the behavioral options (Fredrickson & Branigan, 2005). They foster intuition (Bolte, Goschkey, & Kuhl, 2003) and creativity (Isen, Daubman, & Nowicki, 1987). To summarize, positivity fosters hope, cognitive flexibility, attention span, intuition, and creativity. Do those sound like traits you'd like in your class? See figure 2.2 for an example of positive and negative class cultures.

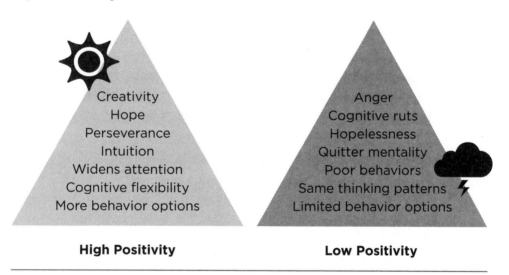

Creativity	Anger
Hope	Cognitive ruts
Perseverance	Hopelessness
Intuition	Quitter mentality
Widens attention	Poor behaviors
Cognitive flexibility	Same thinking patterns
More behavior options	Limited behavior options
High Positivity	**Low Positivity**

Figure 2.2: High positivity versus low positivity.

You may be thinking that a positive mindset will never go over well with your students. But you'd be mistaken. We can learn a positive mindset as a type of *cognitive control* (versus feeling like a victim without choices). This trait (or lack thereof) makes a significant difference in the brains of students from poverty (Noble, Norman, et al., 2005; Noble, Tottenham, & Casey, 2005). How do we know this?

Researchers tested whether ninety-four students at an urban, high-poverty public middle school could learn and actually apply a metacognitive strategy for positivity (Noble, Norman, et al., 2005; Noble, Tottenham, et al., 2005). There were two groups:

one control and one experimental group. The researchers taught students in the experimental group how to convert positive thoughts and images about a desired future (goals) into a self-regulated behavior change (that is, cognitive self-control). It's a simple but powerful strategy consisting of goals, implementation intentions, and a plan of overcoming obstacles.

Over four consecutive quarters, students in the experimental group improved their report card grades, attendance, and even classroom conduct compared with students from the control group (Duckworth, Kirby, Gollwitzer, & Oettingen, 2013). These findings suggest emotional and cognitive control strategies hold considerable promise for helping disadvantaged students improve their academic performance.

Students are powerfully affected when you teach positivity. Frequent positive emotions support a defense against adversity (Fredrickson, Tugade, Waugh, & Larkin, 2003). Pause for a moment; how much of the day do your students spend feeling positive? A positive classroom environment can reduce your primary stress indicators like cortisol (Steptoe, Wardle, & Marmot, 2005). Increasing the neurotransmitter for positive affect (dopamine) leads to strong improvements in learning (Knecht et al., 2004). In short, a positive classroom helps your students behave better and improve their mindsets. It paves the way for them to achieve more.

But there's an even more compelling reason to raise the positivity level. Any high-anticipation goal stimulates our brains to produce noradrenaline and dopamine, the positive neurotransmitters of anticipation of excitement and pleasure (Fredrickson et al., 2003). You don't actually need to reach the goal to feel good (although it's nice). This is why highly motivating and challenging classrooms work.

Remember, you are more than what your genes dictate. Simply put, DNA is not your destiny. You have about twenty thousand genes, many of which the environment can influence (Clamp et al., 2007). So what's the relevance of this number? You have fewer genes than a grape plant or a chicken (thirty thousand–plus genes each), yet the human species built the Egyptian pyramids, space shuttles, the Great Wall of China, and the iPhone. Once again, a student's genes are not his or her destiny. This is true for you too.

Epigenetics, the capacity of the environment to impact genes, is revolutionizing how we see the nature-versus-nurture debate. This capacity allows the environment to influence whether a gene stays silent (suppressed) or becomes turned on (activated). In fact, chronic stress is an example of an everyday experience for your students that can and does influence gene suppression. For example, childhood trauma increases the risk of bipolar disorder (Aas et al., 2016). That's why it's important to be empathetic. This is powerful science that backs up the impact of the positivity mindset and the upbeat classroom climate.

A comprehensive meta-analysis of 121 studies examined the associations between racial discrimination and mental health (such as depression and anxiety), lack of well-being, and physical health. Racial discrimination was present in 76 percent of all adverse outcomes (Priest et al., 2013). The daily effort to deal with being called a minority (someone "less than") as well as seeing the middle class and upper class as unlikely paths are debilitating stressors for many people (Berger & Sarnyai, 2015). That negativity is often reality, and hope is rare. If you truly want students to succeed in a middle- or upper-class world, help them develop the psyche to survive and thrive. That's why it is so critical that you infuse your classroom with daily hope and optimism. Saying, "I will influence student attitudes" is critical for their success.

The Impact of Positivity on the Brain

Fortunately, the positivity mindset is teachable. You can learn it, and you can teach it to your students. In a powerful study of ninety-six diverse schools with a random sample of teachers, positivity makes a significant contribution to student achievement. The research focused on developing classroom optimism. Any teacher who said things like, "You're not going to get an A in my class," acted counter to the research. This study factors in controls for demographic variables and prior student achievement (Hoy, Tarter, & Hoy, 2006), and the students still did better than before with their new mindset. Another study finds a long-term positive behavior intervention changes into a positive thinking-skills intervention (Cohn & Fredrickson, 2010).

Another study uses two existing positive interventions that increase general happiness (gratitude and acts of kindness) in an academic context. These positive psychological interventions fostered positive emotions and improved academic engagement (Barbarin et al., 2013). Whenever students feel better emotionally, good things happen.

Biologically, two neurotransmitters are associated with improved affect: dopamine and serotonin. Both of these, when maintained at moderate levels, have important functions in the school context. For example, higher dopamine levels lead to greater learning (Volkow et al., 2004), working memory (Shellshear et al., 2015), cognitive flexibility (van Holstein et al., 2011), and effort (Beierholm et al., 2013). Do those sound like qualities you'd like in your classroom? You can bump up your students' dopamine production with voluntary gross motor activity, novelty, surprising and fun activities, and anticipation of a rewarding event.

Serotonin levels are associated with other good outcomes: increased production of new brain cells (Klanker, Feenstra, & Denys, 2013) and better attention, learning, mood regulation, and long-term memory (Meneses & Liy-Salmeron, 2012). You can increase your students' serotonin production in a classroom with increased calmness, feelings of control, and the use of predictable rituals, camaraderie, and cooperation—a safe environment. You may guess that your class needs some of each, dopamine and serotonin.

Your brain does not produce them at the same time, so your teaching can help you use the energy of novelty and the calmness of predictability. Healthy classrooms have a rhythm to them, moving from novelty to predictability.

Noradrenaline is a powerful neurotransmitter that can foster better focus and long-term memory (Hurlemann et al., 2005). Fast energizers, high levels of urgency, excitement, and perception of risk stimulate increased noradrenaline. For example, when students present in front of their peers under a deadline, they feel urgency, excitement, and at risk. Your teaching influences the production of several neurotransmitters. You have more to do with how your students behave than you previously thought. See figure 2.3 for how these slow-acting chemicals affect your class.

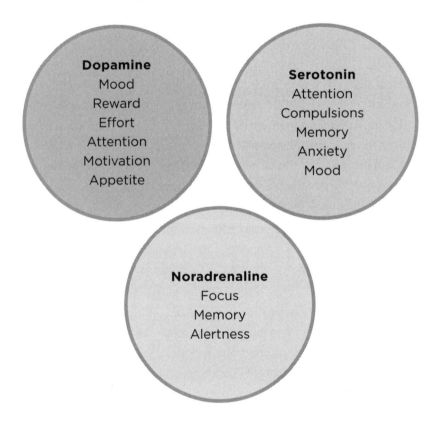

Your actions and words influence each of these.

Figure 2.3: How brain chemicals change your class.

Noradrenaline, dopamine, and serotonin are just a few of the neurotransmitters at work in your students' brains while you're teaching. You need them on your side to succeed at your job. The point is, don't look at your class and think the students are being negative. Roll up your sleeves and influence how your students feel. The evidence is on your side.

Quick Consolidation

I introduced you to the science behind classroom feelings because many of these causes and effects are invisible to the untrained eye. Now you know *why* it is so important for students to want to be in your class. You're now getting a sense of the deep levels of change that come about when students feel good in class and school. The content you're required to teach will always be in transition; changing standards are a given. The one reliable, unstoppable force in your class must be *you* using a positive attitude, tone, climate, and sky-high expectations each day. In the following four chapters, you'll read about four strategies to promote a positivity mindset in your classroom.

1. Boost optimism and hope.
2. Build positive attitudes.
3. Foster control, choice, and relevancy.
4. Change the emotional set point.

Positive affect in school contributes to more kindness, better health, increased participation, fewer absences, and greater achievement. Turn to the next chapter to learn how to boost optimism and hope every day.

CHAPTER 3

BOOST OPTIMISM AND HOPE

The positivity mindset focuses on building both optimism and hope. I'm inviting you to focus this year on building these traits in students because they may ensure your students' success well beyond graduation. You'll be developing positivity, hopefulness, and a sense of capacity for lifelong challenges. Those underpinnings of a solid life can make a positive attitude become real. Your positivity needs a basis; you must sustain it and continually find the hidden goodness in nearly everything.

You'll want to provide both the academic and life skills to sustain hope and optimism. Here you'll learn some of the proven ways you can start this process with your students.

Teach Optimism and Hope Building

Optimism and hope are different. Hope is an orientation of spirit. It is the certainty that something will ultimately take a turn for the better, regardless of the outcome. A hopeful person often has a low level of personal control and yet lives knowing that his or her life is in good hands (Bruininks & Malle, 2005). This is relevant; because the poor often feel less in control, building hope is powerful.

Optimism requires a belief that things will get better due to the efficacy of one's own progress (Bailey, Eng, Frisch, & Snyder, 2007). It is also about perspective; one can learn to see the good side of nearly any event or person. Optimism and hope are both teachable traits (Seligman, 2006). Optimistic students with hope are more cheerful and

23

work harder. They make teaching more fun and perform better. If you don't teach this, who will? See table 3.1 for what hope and optimism sound like.

Table 3.1: Differentiating Hope and Optimism

Hope	Optimism
"I know good things will happen. It will all turn out for the better."	"Due to the efficacy of my own progress, things will get better."
"Bad things have happened before; I'm sure it will be all right in the end."	"I learned what I did wrong in the past. I know just what to change, so I think it will be better tomorrow."
"Some things we just don't have control over. We just have to trust everything's going to be OK."	"I have been working on this for a while. I think I got it right. Next week, it's going to be amazing."

You are about to read some simple, easy-to-implement classroom strategies. These may seem very familiar to you. They may trigger memories of strategies you have heard of or may have used before. But knowing about a strategy does not raise student achievement. I have a simple request for you. Read each as if it is the very first time. Then, ask yourself, "Am I actually doing this on a daily basis to the best of my ability?"

Here are your four strategies for optimism and hope.

1. Model optimism daily.
2. Build hope daily.
3. Build students' self-concept and effort levels.
4. Develop hope relentlessly.

Model Optimism Daily

When you are optimistic, you believe there are no negative events. You simply think that most negative events are temporary, limited, and manageable. Notice how this model also assumes you can take potential action to ensure you will survive. For many students, optimism is the only way they can begin to see the world differently. Model optimism for students every day in every way you can think of. Your smile, confidence, and energy are powerful. Roll up your sleeves and start showing your students the life skills to have a great day, every day. When a student asks, "How ya doing?" answer with phrases like, "Never been better," "I'm living my dream," or "It's a great day to learn!" Then, add, "And, how about you?" Show them what it's like to love your job and help others and how to ignore the negativity of bad news. Be the model of the teacher who loves teaching. Modeled optimism can be contagious. Consider the following strategies.

Teaching Perspective

Perspective helps students gain the real power of optimism. Teach your students how, upon hearing or reading a news story, to look at different sides of it. For example, say the headline reads, "Six inches of snow predicted tomorrow; school will be closed!" Ask students who would be happy about this and who the weather might hurt.

Simple activities in which students take different sides of a topic help them build alternate points of view and see the positives in each situation. In this activity, two students pair up, and the teacher gives a scenario. You might try scenarios like these.

- You got a low score on a test. How could you use this to your advantage?

- You didn't get accepted to your first choice for college. How could that be a good thing?

- You didn't get the job you wanted. How could that be a positive thing?

Students alternate giving pros and cons. Share a few examples from your own life to make the activity real to them. Invite questions so students start to process this internally.

Using Word Nutrients

As a role model for students, choose words that are like supplements to students' brains. Word nutrients are daily words and actions that feed positive attitudes. Be sure to share the "seed of something greater" attitude with your students. When students enter the room, instead of saying "Hi," say, "It's stupendous to see you today!"

Word nutrients are also part of a powerful writing activity. Here's how it works.

1. Students brainstorm ten positive words or phrases as a class.
2. Then, students write for three to five minutes about something good that happened last week.
3. Then, they write about something troubling to them. When students reflect on mistakes or bad things, it is a good, diffusing activity (Lyubomirsky, Sousa, & Dickerhoof, 2006).
4. Finally, ask students to choose a positive word for the day and use it at least five more times that day.

Do not grade these; the very act of writing about their lives has been shown to be positive (Lyubomirsky et al., 2006).

Overcoming Setbacks

All of us fail. What counts is what we do after we fail. When you fall down, get up. That's the secret; never give up. Give classroom examples of how you have done this in the past. Then, have students share examples with the whole class, and ask, "How will you deal with it?"

Using quick-writes is a powerful way to help students understand themselves and see the world differently. Have students write for three to ten minutes on overcoming setbacks, such as "How might I solve a problem I'm having?" "How can I improve my grade on an upcoming test?" It's important for students to reflect on times where they've failed but refused to quit.

Let them start the process of problem solving instead of feeling powerless. Most important, allow students to share what they wrote in small groups or in front of the class.

There are countless resources available for building a positive, behavior-changing daily attitude with your students. One of my favorites is Jack Canfield's (2015) *The Success Principles*. Most of the chapters are just five to ten pages. Read just one chapter per week. Take what you read and adapt it for your students. You can foster the positivity to overcome setbacks. See figure 3.1 for a sample poster to hang in your classroom.

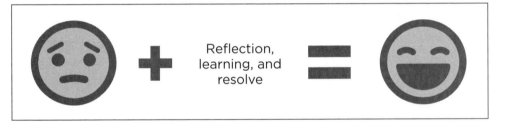

Figure 3.1: Overcoming setbacks.

Build Hope Daily

Building hope daily is not a check-the-box activity. This is a constant process of instilling a lifelong sense of possibility for something good. Begin with building a relationship based on respect and empathy for your students. This alone can create hope. Now, here are some specific strategies to build hope over time. You'll want students to practice new skills in class weekly, so they see that they are growing and improving.

Giving Daily Affirmations

Every day, affirm your students' goodness, positive energy, and success, and work to create a classroom climate where peers do the same to each other. Encourage your students to turn to their neighbors and say things like, "You're on fire today!" "You rock!" "Love your attitude, girl!" Getting peer and teacher affirmation are hope builders.

Teaching Goal Setting

Teach your students to set daily, weekly, and yearly goals. Make progress visible; it may inspire students. Teach students how to assess progress, get feedback, and correct their courses in order to score higher. Give each student a handout (or use a tablet) with room for his or her weekly, monthly, and annual goals. Underneath the long-term goals, students can write their weekly goals and strategies. Managing your destiny is a hope builder. Visit **go.SolutionTree.com/instruction** for the online-only reproducible "Managing My Destiny."

Encouraging Dreams

Ask for your students' dreams and visions of their own future. Help them find their voices, paths, and strengths. Consider asking the following introspective questions to get students to think about the future and current strengths.

- What would make my own life amazingly great?
- Where do I want to be in five, ten, or even fifteen years?
- What am I already good at?
- How could I help others?
- What kind of person do I want to be?
- What would I be doing?
- Who would I need to help me?
- What do I need to get there?
- When will I start reaching my dreams?

You affirm their dreams when you allow them to draw, sing, or share with others. Instill a class rule: "No dream killers." As students share their dreams with others, they may or may not get peer approval. But they will get support from their teacher—you! Fostering dreams is a hope builder.

Displaying Daily Progress

Continually point out and display progress. Students need to see that they are improving and getting closer to their goals, or they may give up on themselves. Post class progress reports (as a whole) and team progress reports. Getting better is a hope builder.

Sharing Success Stories

Success stories are important. Show and tell them stories of students just like them who have already made it and how they made it. Google "amazing students" or "teens who make a difference," and there are thousands of students who are already changing the world. One fifth-grade teacher had banners from universities from all over the country on the walls of his classroom. Underneath each college banner were the real names of former students from his class who went to that college. Seeing real results from your own class is a hope builder.

Finding a Cause

Help students find a cause where they can donate their time or expertise to others. At age nine, Katie Stagliano started donating vegetables to homeless kitchens. Today, her organization, Katie's Krops (www.katieskrops.com), helps thousands. This service can help the elderly, a charity, or an individual student with unusual challenges. For many, it becomes a life-changing experience. Helping others is an empowering hope builder.

Assigning Real-World Jobs

Ensure that all jobs that students do at school have real-world job titles. Even for first graders, never give students a job title like *line leader*. Have you ever, in your lifetime, had a student come up to you and say, "When I grow up, I want to be a line leader"? Of course not! Raise the bar for expectations. Change every classroom job into a real-world job. For example:

- Line leader = tour guide
- Bathroom monitor = security
- Pet keeper = zoologist
- Paper monitor = materials handler or logistics
- Aquarium keeper = marine biologist
- Caboose = security

Connecting school to the real world and careers is a hope builder.

Including Affirmations of Hope

Class posters and placards should contain affirmations of hope (for example, "The harder I work, the luckier I get"), and students should read books about hope and successful role models. For example, consider A Mighty Girl (www.amightygirl.com) books, which focus on girl-led titles for all ages.

Each day, a different student can be responsible for writing and sharing a positive affirmation for the class. Keep these fresh, and rotate them around the room. Over time, let students contribute their own affirmations. Affirming capacity is a hope builder. See figure 3.2 for a sample class poster including an affirmation of hope.

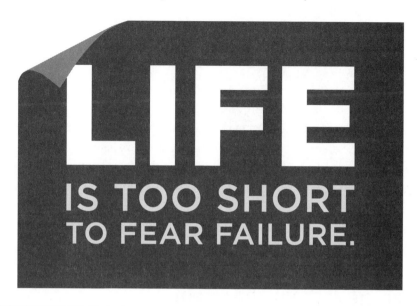

Figure 3.2: Sample class poster.

*Visit **go.SolutionTree.com/instruction** for a reproducible version of this figure.*

Build Students' Self-Concept and Effort Levels

Most teachers who struggle with students will tell you that their students act out in class, don't do their homework, are disrespectful, and are often tardy. Now ask the high-performing teacher what's wrong with those same students, and you'll hear, "I love my students! They work hard, work together, and are getting better every week." What's different: the students?

No, strong teachers purposefully *choose* to affirm student strengths. They choose to build student self-concept and effort levels. The struggling teachers choose to break down students, making them feel small by pointing out their flaws (as if no one else has flaws). To help your students grow, make it your mission to find and develop their strengths. This does not mean you are blind to their weaknesses. It means building them up enough that they can deal with error corrections and helpful feedback. Here's how you can do it.

Using a Power Minute

At least once a week (it's usually best on a Monday or Friday), have students share something about themselves in a *power minute*. Consider the following topics.

- One strength they have
- Someone they care about
- Someone they have helped recently

- Something they admire in others
- How they helped a friend lately
- A goal or milestone they have reached lately

Don't ask all students to share in a single day; stretch the activity out over a few months. To keep the activity fresh, rotate how you do it, and keep the sharing under four minutes. For example, students can share in four ways: (1) on paper or in a journal, (2) to their study buddy, (3) within a cooperative learning group or team, or (4) with the whole class. Remember to respect their privacy, and give them time to become comfortable with these powerful self-affirmations. Also, remember to praise effort, choices, strategies, and attitudes, as a student can manage each of these. Never praise or showboat about a student's intelligence or how smart he or she is, as this is an ineffective form of feedback (Mueller & Dweck, 1998; Rattan, Savani, Chugh, & Dweck, 2015).

Listening Without Judgment

Teach others (and yourself) to listen without judgment. Be the listener that you wish others would have been for you as a student. Sometimes students are clumsy at giving feedback, but they still have useful things to say. Listen past the negative feelings, and ask yourself, "Is there anything I can learn from what this student said?"

In short, before you react, get defensive, or get angry, pause to listen. Search for the most actionable jewel of change. Ask yourself, "Can I learn anything, even if it's what not to do?" This attitude of always learning will help your students grow. For example, if a student says, "You don't make any sense," take the feedback as a gift. Say, "I'm sorry. Would you suggest I say it differently, go slower, or maybe draw it out?"

Affirming Student Strengths With a Connection

Use attribution in your affirmations. Attribution is connecting the cause and effect of an action to the outcome. Always affirm their strengths *with a connection*. It's not enough to say, "Eric, you really write well" (Rattan et al., 2015). Say, "Eric, when you add practical strategies, I understand better what you are talking about. Plus, that strategy will help with your dream of publishing a book."

It's also helpful to make the connection as detailed as possible: "Eric, I like how you supported your argument here in this paragraph with evidence. That skill may help you reach your goal of being an author." When students hear you (as an authority figure) affirm their effort and connect it to how that strength will do some good in the world, students take more pride in their strengths and work harder.

One thing to keep in mind is how much a student's understanding of effort and ability is dependent on age. Nicholls and Miller (1984) describe four levels of attribution theory.

- **Level 1 (from five to six years old):** Students do not understand the difference between effort and ability or cause and effect.

- **Level 2 (from seven to nine years old):** Students attribute outcome purely to effort.
- **Level 3 (from ten to eleven years old):** Students can distinguish between ability and effort but will often still mix them up.
- **Level 4 (twelve years and older):** Students clearly understand the difference between effort and ability.

While attributing a success or failure to a trait that we have some control over (like effort, attitude, or strategy) remember to ensure your comments are developmentally appropriate.

Creating a Classroom Directory

Some teachers help students create a classroom version of Facebook, where students list two to three of their strengths and include details about their friends and family so the class gets a sense of who they are. This class directory can be a three-ring binder or posted online to the classroom webpage of the school's site. Using this information, some teachers create a classroom experts directory, so students know who to go to when they need help. Students can be the in-house experts on fixing technology, clothes purchases, trivia, sports, games, and yes, even classroom content.

Develop Hope Relentlessly

In figure 2.1 (page 16), you saw that the poor hear far more negative comments at home than the middle or upper class. Many students have also learned how to become defensive and sarcastic from their teachers. Please refrain from using the following negative expressions, and consider the positive alternatives.

- **Old way:** "How about if you show up on time tomorrow, for a change?"

  Positive way: "You've been on time twice this week. I love seeing you on time!"

- **Old way:** "Shock me, and bring in some homework tomorrow."

  Positive way: "Eric, I would love to see your homework tomorrow. I'm hoping you remember that your homework is not graded. I just want you to take a few minutes to practice what we do in class. It helps your brain sort out the learning and save it for later."

- **Old way:** "You are doing it this way because I said so!"

  Positive way: "We do this because it is safer, and it includes everyone else in the room."

- **Old way:** "Eyes up here! I want everyone to see how Eric is sitting up straight, ready to learn. You all please do this too." (Students dislike being compared to other students.)

  Positive way: "Right now, we've got 40, 50, now we're already at 60 percent and going higher with a great ready-to-learn posture. Let's keep going to 100 percent."

- **Old way:** "You're never going to graduate. Not with how (lazy, stubborn, annoying, or tardy) you've been in my class."

  Positive way: "Could you hang out for just a moment after class?" Then, after class, you say, "I like having you in my class. Have you ever thought about what you want to be doing in five, ten, or fifteen years? Maybe we can take a few moments on another day and flesh out some ideas. Are you OK with that?"

Consider using such positive sentiments with the following strategies.

Supporting Dreams

Why not ask students what they want to be doing ten years after they graduate? You have no idea who a student might become. Consider Monty, a high school student from Salinas, California (Canfield & Hansen, 2013). It is a predominately low-income area, where most of the employment is in agriculture. In English class, his teacher asked him to write about his life dream for ten years after graduation. Monty wrote a seven-page paper, detailing how he wanted to own a two hundred–acre ranch with a four thousand–square-foot house where he could train thoroughbreds. His teacher gave him an F on the paper. Why? He said that his dream was unrealistic (after all, he was poor). The teacher told Monty that part of the assignment was to be practical, and his dream was totally impractical. He offered Monty a chance to rewrite his paper. After thinking about it overnight and talking it over with his dad, Monty returned to class and told his teacher, "I'll tell you what; you keep the F, and I'll keep my dream." When students do share dreams, don't criticize or judge them; accept and support them.

By the way, Monty did get his dream. Today, he owns a two hundred–acre ranch in Solvang, California, where he raises and trains thoroughbreds as well as offers training for other horse trainers from around the world. Monty is the original horse whisperer. He does have a four thousand–square-foot house and has written multiple bestsellers. He has trained horses from royalty, and a movie was made about his life. Not bad for a student whose teacher thought his dreams were too big. What would you say to a student of yours who wants to be a billionaire, rap mogul, president, doctor, neuroscientist, or astronaut? Here's the right answer: "I love your dream! Let's sit down and make a plan."

Building Strong Relationships

Relationships matter. Very few things foster hope and optimism for students like quality relationships with adults. Healthy relationships allow each party to see that they are worthy and capable. Strong adult role models can be the rock in a student's life. I am absolutely sold on the power of relationships because they are what changed my own life. Here are the five best areas to target relationships at your school.

1. **Teacher to student:** Learn three things about every student besides his or her name. Make each student, even the most difficult one, into your greatest ally with friendship and listening. Ask students to write a paragraph titled, "What I wish my teacher knew about me."

2. **Teacher to teacher:** Work to create a schoolwide culture of friendship, trust, and collaboration. Use these magic phrases with other staff: "I am sorry," "I appreciate what you did," "I agree with your premise," "Thank you so much," "Can I give you a hand?," "It was my mistake. How can I make it right?," and "I respect what you did."

3. **Student to student:** Set a weekly target to make 50 percent or more of student time collaborative. This can help students make more of an effort and improve their behavior and achievement. Because affiliation and status seeking are important to students, collaboration can allow for both. Ensure students have mentors, study buddies, and teams to work with. Help each student feel like an important part of your class with inclusion, roles, and support. Start the year with get-to-know-you activities, and use names in class to build camaraderie and teamwork. Have students write a one-page paper on "What I wish other students knew about me."

4. **Staff to the community:** In the first four to six weeks of school, visit the homes of your students. When staff do this, it's a way of saying to parents, "You're important, and your child is important." At the secondary level, select one to three students from each class to visit.

5. **Teacher to parents:** Be part of the Parent/Teacher Home Visit Project (www.pthvp.org). When your school commits to this, you are likely to see miracles. Parents are usually blown away when a teacher visits their home. It shows the teacher's depth of care, and as a result, the parent often reciprocates. Does your school offer events that parents and others in the community may be interested in, such as arts performances, science fairs, and parent workshops on how to help children succeed? Start up a weekly Parent University, and help parents "graduate" from your school with new parenting strategies, cooking ideas, stress tools, and other skills to make their lives easier.

Quick Consolidation

I have come to understand why daily optimism and positive energy work so well. It's more than engagement. It's more than a coping tool or happy face in the classroom. Teachers who build a positivity mindset rewire their students' brains in profound ways, even affecting their genes (Fredrickson & Losada, 2005).

You learned several ways to strengthen students' points of view and daily positive outlooks. For many students, losing hope means the game is over—students may drop out. What you have seen so far is this: students do not create their own attitudes in a vacuum. They get them from others, including you. The good news is that you have students in a nearly perfect situation (trapped, in a good way) to influence their brains. Use these positive strategies every day, and you'll start seeing and hearing positive students over time. Your own attitude should be, "Take charge; my students are going to develop great attitudes, and positivity will come from me every day!"

Where can you start today?

CHAPTER 4

BUILD POSITIVE ATTITUDES

The transformation of your classroom culture continues with a look at some research on building positive attitudes. We started with boosting skills that have a strong research base: optimism and hope. Now, we build on those traits with a focus not on oneself but on others. These are social traits that change lives.

- Gratitude building
- Service work and acts of kindness
- Personal responsibility and self-regulation

Gratitude Building

Let's start with gratitude building. Occasionally, teachers raise their eyebrows when I talk about gratitude, as if they think that gratitude is something only the elderly ask of their grandchildren: "Be grateful for what you have!" Actually, it is a transformative human trait, and here's the research that proves how powerful it is.

In a study with 221 early adolescents, having a grateful outlook was associated with enhanced self-reported optimism and life satisfaction and decreased negative affect. The most significant finding is the robust relationship between gratitude and satisfaction with school experience (Froh, Sefick, & Emmons, 2008). This is the key for you; model an attitude of gratitude. Gratitude affirms what we experience is good. Through gratitude, we see there are good things in the world. Gratitude grants a gift to those receiving it and invites us to see how others have supported us. This makes gratitude both personal and social. Studies suggest that this "find, remind, and bind" attitude that is part of gratitude can change your life (and your students' lives) for the better. In our relationships, it's important we remind others of our gratitude, which helps us connect better (Algoe, 2012). Most of your students have not yet learned this skill. Yet, this gratitude-building process builds new brain pathways that protect us all from stress and negativity by fostering relationships and appreciation (Algoe, Haidt, & Gable, 2008). Let's begin by building an emotional bank account stacked with gratitude. See figure 4.1.

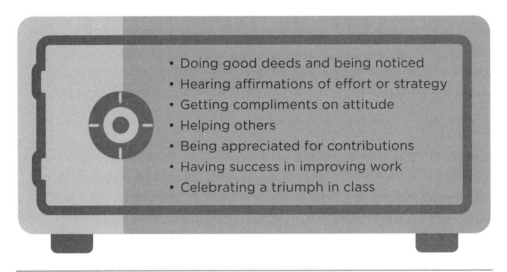

- Doing good deeds and being noticed
- Hearing affirmations of effort or strategy
- Getting compliments on attitude
- Helping others
- Being appreciated for contributions
- Having success in improving work
- Celebrating a triumph in class

Figure 4.1: The emotional bank account.

To start building this emotional bank account every day, share with your students something that you are grateful for (your health, family, job, friends, the weather, and so on). Students need to see an adult showing gratitude; if you're not grateful, they're less likely to buy into the attitude they need to learn.

Your openness will, over time, help students to become more comfortable sharing their gratitude with others. If your students like and respect you, they're more likely to see building gratitude as something good that they'd like to try out. An expert in gratitude at the University of California, Davis, shares these research-based tips for your gratitude process (Emmons, 2007; Sheldon & Lyubomirsky, 2006). Share them with students.

- **Keep it personal:** Focusing on people to whom you are grateful has more of a positive impact than focusing on things for which you are grateful. Think about others' support, sacrifices, and contributions.

- **Start with a goal:** Set a positive, grateful goal in a personal or classroom journal. Motivation to become more satisfied and joyful helps add value to the journaling.

- **Favor depth over breadth:** Elaborating deeply about one thing is better than glossing over many things. Focus on what is surprising and unexpected. Think of facts about your life, such as advantages and opportunities.

- **Use a take-away-the-goodness strategy:** Reflect on what your life would be like *without* a certain positive event (versus all the positives).

- **Reflect on the good things weekly:** Writing once a week will facilitate greater boosts in happiness than writing three times per week (Sheldon & Lyubomirsky, 2006). As your brain adapts, when you expect a good thing every day, it can lose its impact. "Let's journal about one thing that happened this week at school for which we're thankful."

- **Keep the gratitude process fresh:** Once students have learned to share daily gratitude, mix up the process, using the following five strategies.

  a. *Sharing with a buddy*—Students share their feelings of gratitude with a partner.

  b. *Using a journal*—Students write their feelings of gratitude in a gratitude journal.

  c. *Starting small*—Students share just one small thing (in detail) that they are grateful for with a peer.

  d. *Sharing in a circle*—Students share in a small circle, which affirms the value of gratitude. After each speaks, others thank him or her. This reinforcement establishes that gratitude is good, especially when it's shared, which creates group norms.

  e. *Making a poster*—Students can work with a partner or a small team to create a poster. Alternatively, create a gratitude poster that students can add to over time. Students sign it, see it, and take pride in it (see figure 4.2, page 38).

Never think that student attitudes are outside your influence. You can and do influence them every day. But beware: if you do one of the gratitude activities as a simple time filler, you are highly unlikely to get any good out of it. Make the activity happen for five to seven minutes a day, three times a week, for two to six months. Constantly tweak the activity to keep it fresh with just enough novelty to prevent student boredom. Increase the challenge and complexity of the activity so the process becomes a worthwhile mental journey instead of a mindless routine.

Now we'll take a look at how service work and acts of kindness support the positivity mindset.

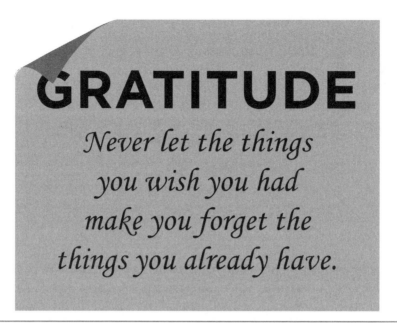

Figure 4.2: Sample gratitude poster.

Service Work and Acts of Kindness

Research shows that daily acts of kindness create changes in the lives of the giver and receiver (Otake, Shimai, Tanaka-Matsumi, Otsui, & Fredrickson, 2006). In fact, kind people experience more happiness (Otake et al., 2006). Many programs that build student character include the simple strategy to help students become net *givers* instead of net *takers*.

One study found that the biggest boost in happiness was when people piled up three to five acts in one day instead of stretching them out over time (Layous & Lyubomirsky, 2014). Pick just one day a week for extra kindnesses like those mentioned in this section. This experience seems to intensify positive emotions, creating a much greater emotional high. See figure 4.3.

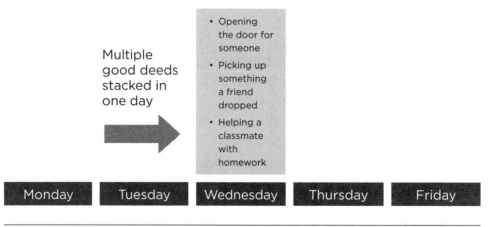

Figure 4.3: Stack up the kindness.

Service Work

Service work means simply doing public work. Why would students want to do this? Read "12 Reasons Community Service Should Be Required in Schools" (Online College, 2012) to learn the benefits of community service for students.

Where would you or your students start? Use the following as sources for ideas.

- **Local and national news:** Look for the stories on existing projects that others are doing, like a book drive. Many of them could use help.

- **Local animal shelters:** Volunteers are used for animal support tasks, such as cleaning cages, answering phones, or making shelter waiting rooms a nicer area.

- **Parks, community orchards, and beaches:** Environments always have needs that students can fill. Students can plant trees, clean up unsightly areas, or do beach trash pickups.

- **Seniors and nursing homes:** Many senior citizens would relish the time and help as would a private nursing home where volunteers are also needed. Contact the recreation director who plans activities.

- **Agencies:** During the holidays, students can work with agencies that need temporary help. There are many agencies that need food or gifts for deserving families. Your students can ask for donations.

- **Military families:** Look up organizations that ship packages to troops, such as Operation Gratitude (www.operationgratitude.com) or Operation Troop Support (http://operationtroopsupport.org). Get donations and support our troops.

Look for agencies that experience pervasive challenges, for example, shelters that feed the homeless daily need fresh vegetables. This problem is something that a school can eliminate by raising crops and donating the vegetables. (Visit http://katieskrops.com to learn how one child began growing and donating fresh cabbage to a local soup kitchen and how others have joined her.) If your students want to broaden their reach, visit www .dosomething.org/us/campaigns to read about what others are doing and find an already operating campaign. (Visit **go.SolutionTree.com/instruction** to access live links to the websites mentioned in this book.)

Acts of Kindness

In a study of nineteen elementary classrooms, researchers asked students to perform three acts of kindness per week over the course of four weeks. Students who did so experienced significant increases in peer acceptance, which translated to better behaviors

(Layous, Nelson, Oberle, Schonert-Reichl, & Lyubomirsky, 2012). This sounds good, but what about adolescents?

At the secondary level, another study had similarly good findings: students who engaged in daily acts of kindness behaved better in school and strengthened their resolve to improve academically (Ouweneel, Le Blanc, & Schaufeli, 2014). Acts of kindness are easy; simply invite students to try these out while at school.

Consider using the Magic Three strategy and creating lists to stack up your acts of kindness.

The Magic Three

The Magic Three strategy uses the words *respect*, *agree*, and *appreciate* to defuse and de-escalate any situation. When a student experiences conflict, students start arguing, or a student starts shouting or gets upset, here's what to do. Remember, others need to feel that their voices are heard first.

1. If you want them to listen, you go first and say, "I *respect* (your right to say that, your feelings, the work you put in, your passion, or how you feel about that)."

2. You can also say, "I *agree* with (your position, strategy, understanding of the topic, or problems)." You may not agree with their strategy, but you can agree with their intention (the need to change a rule or system).

3. Finally, you can say, "I *appreciate* (the hard work you put in, the way you care about this, your commitment, or you wanting to talk this through)."

Notice how these openings—*respect*, *agree*, and *appreciate*—slow things down, soften the tone, and let the student know that you do see good in him or her. Once students feel they've had a chance to be heard, you can have a much more productive (and less combative) conversation.

Acts-of-Kindness Lists

Empower students to create their own acts-of-kindness lists so they can do the things they've chosen for themselves. Here are some suggestions to help students get started.

- Letting another student go ahead of you in line
- Taking garbage to the trash can
- Sharing a favorite song
- Helping someone at lunch
- Helping a friend fix something
- Helping another student with homework
- Sharing food or movie ideas
- Getting a tissue for someone who needs it (like after a sneeze)

Ensure students acknowledge each other publicly (if they give permission) as well as privately for their kind deeds. Over time, this will not just help students feel better about themselves but just may transform your school culture.

Next, we look at the role of personal responsibility in building attitudes of gratitude and contributing to the positivity mindset.

Personal Responsibility and Self-Regulation

Many truisms become part of people for so long that it is easy to forget how powerful they are and the effect they have. For example, it's likely that years ago, someone said to you (or you figured out), "It's not what happens to you in life that shapes your future, it is how you deal with what happens."

In other words, you're not always responsible for what happens to you in life. But you sure are responsible for how you respond to what happens. You will feel frustrated, receive criticism, fall down, get hurt, fail, and endure bad luck. There's no shortage of real-world examples. When Amy Purdy (Amy Purdy, n.d.) was nineteen, she contracted meningococcal meningitis. She lost her spleen, kidney function, the hearing in her left ear, and, due to septic shock, both of her legs below the knee. But, as I've stated, Amy realized she wasn't responsible for what happened to her. She wasn't going to shrink from life. As a double amputee, Amy became a Paralympic snowboarder, a best-selling author, motivational speaker, clothing designer, and an inspiration on *Dancing With the Stars*. When bad things happen to you, say, "Welcome to the club called humanity." We all experience our unique lives, full of pain and joy. Amy's attitude helped her be a success.

When you learn to regulate your intentions, you become a player, not a bystander. You become a force to be reckoned with because you manage your emotions and have a better work ethic. Your students can deal with this process by mastering how to run their own brains, learn from real-world examples, reframe to stay positive, handle negatives constructively, and choose their battles.

Running Your Own Brain

An important way for students to take personal responsibility over their actions and commit to a positive mindset is learning how to run their own brains. Simply teach your students the following skills. (See appendix B, page 163, for a more in-depth look at running your own brain.)

- Share with your students simple strategies to de-stress (tense up and release, take a walk, take slow deep breaths, or redirect attention to something more fun).

- Teach students how to resist bad temptations (distract yourself, reframe it, move your feet quickly past the situation, or have a prepared way of saying *no*).

- Coach students on how to deal with bad feelings (talk it out with a friend, go work out, write out how you feel, or take time to reflect on whether reconciliation is possible).

- Instruct students how to deal with negative feedback. If you don't teach them how to respond, they'll never get better (take some time to sort it out and ask for suggestions to improve).

- Teach students how to engage in constructive self-talk. Role model it, and then give them a weekly assignment with a partner ("Man, I let myself fall behind, but I have to get caught up. I have to start a new habit today" or "I feel bad I forgot about my assignment. I should've written it down. I need to make an effort to write down everything I have to do").

Another way students can run their own brains is through self-regulation. Teach students the following skills.

- Resisting impulsivity
- Assuming good in others
- Paying lengthy attention
- Learning from mistakes
- Complying with adult requests, as appropriate
- Deferring gratification
- Managing stress
- Managing negative self-talk
- Being patient before getting angry
- Thinking before responding
- Having situational awareness

Role modeling is key to teaching students how to run their own brains. Consider the following teacher-student conversation.

> **Teacher:** You've got a great attitude about learning. What's needed to help get you to proficiency is a more locked in, focused effort until you're done. As I said, you've got a lot going for you. Now, tell me what you heard me say.
>
> **Student:** I heard you say that I ain't working hard enough.

Teacher: That's part of it. I said two things. First, I appreciate your attitude, and I like that about you. Second, a more solid effort will help you get the grades that will help you graduate.

Student: Well, what if I don't care whether I graduate or not?

Teacher: Your high school diploma simply gives you more choices in life. You want your own car? A diploma helps you get the job that buys the car. You may not like certain classes in school, but school helps you develop and nail down habits like everyday attitudes, job skills, people skills, on-time habits, and work effort. In school, we practice learning and accomplishing things. Why? You can use them in your life and get paid for them in your job. Does that make sense?

Student: Yeah, I get it. I just don't feel like doing this.

Teacher: I get it too; that's part of growing up. You won't like everything in the world that you have to do. I don't like washing my car, taking out the trash, or paying bills, but I do it. Tell you what; let's meet for three minutes after class, and I'll help you make a plan that might save you some time. Can you meet me halfway on this?

Learning From Real-World Examples

Share a real-world role model's quote or book with students. Choose someone who takes personal responsibility for his or her actions and writes about how to do that; think again about Amy Purdy (page 41). Your students need to know they are not alone. Successful people have learned to be responsible because that is what works in life.

Reframing to Stay Positive

Teach the skills of reframing to stay positive. Students can learn to say to themselves, "Maybe I am having a bad day" instead of "My life stinks" or "I didn't do well on this test" instead of "I'm an idiot." Find a way, mentally, to refrain from judgment or criticism and instead see another's point of view. Teach students that sometimes the source of the negativity is a constant, and it's best to spend less time around it.

Handling the Negatives Constructively

Post the sign *What to Do When It's Not Working* in your class. The sign should have a simple five-step process that every student can follow: (1) take a deep breath, (2) say "I can do this," (3) list three things to do differently to help lead to success, (4) try out your best of the three choices, and (5) evaluate progress and either continue or go back to step 1. Visit **go.SolutionTree.com/instruction** to download a free reproducible of this sign.

When you criticize a student, often he or she has no clue how to behave or respond. The student may not have been taught the right skills at home, or chronic stress could be dominating his or her behaviors. Neither of those are the student's fault. Stop telling students what to do. Teach them how to behave, or they will counterattack or go silent. Without teaching them how, students will get in trouble over and over and soon the suspensions will follow. Unless you help, they may drop out.

Some students don't have the skills to speak their mind, but it's important for the teacher to stand up for them and be polite and civil about the situation. Encourage upset students to say, "Listen, I am sorry I messed up. I just didn't know what else to do. Help me out, and please tell me what you want me to do instead of telling me what's wrong."

Choosing Your Battles

Teach your students never to argue with a constantly negative or angry person. Role model this with your students. In class, when things get out of hand with a student, simply say, "I respect your point of view and appreciate what you're saying. It does sound like you and I have to sort some things out. Let's do this privately a bit later so the rest of the class can move forward." Otherwise, both of you will end up feeling worse in the end. Listen to what the student said, but if nothing applies to you, let it go. If the shoe fits, pick it up and try it out. If it doesn't, leave it alone. Simply breathe in good thoughts, and breathe out the stress. You and your students have more important things to do.

Quick Consolidation

Every time I read about or visit with high performers, I learn something profound. These teachers are a magnificent walking database of insights and solutions. A surprising focus for these teachers is on the power of emotions and how they impact others. You may be one of many who already tap into this powerful tool. In this chapter, you got several key strategies proven to help students become more positive.

- Gratitude building
- Service work and acts of kindness
- Personal responsibility and self-regulation

After all, no matter how good your students get, unless you help them internalize those strengths and feel good about themselves for a solid reason, they will always have paralyzing doubts that hold them back.

CHAPTER 5

FOSTER CONTROL, CHOICE, AND RELEVANCY

This chapter continues to fill your toolbox with tools for building the positivity mindset. When students are in a positive state of mind, they have fewer behavioral issues and better academic results. Control, choice, and relevancy are core factors that suggest the potency of what I call the *invisible teaching velocity*—a process so subtle that other teachers may miss it when watching rich teaching. It's easy to miss these strategies. Why? They may seem inconsequential, but they are not. When you give students more choice and control over their daily experiences and show them the relevancy of what they're doing, you can reach them emotionally and personally. But why do these three work so well, and why should you care? That's the topic of this chapter, but first you'll want a brief bit of background.

Evidence for Control, Choice, and Relevancy

We have all heard a teacher say that his or her students don't try, work hard, or put out effort. If you've had those thoughts before, this chapter is for you. The three items in the chapter title—(1) control, (2) choice, (3) relevancy—actually occur sequentially in a well-run classroom.

When students feel stressed, they crave control. When my wife gets stressed, she will relish doing housework because it helps her feel some mastery (control) over her life. For me, I do garage and yard work. Having control lowers stress. Once you have control, you want choice.

But not all choice is good choice; it has to be relevant. Let's begin with a review of what is common among students from poverty.

In a classroom at a high-poverty school, you'll often see tense dynamics over classroom control. Teachers want to control their students so they don't get out of line. Students want more control so they are pushing boundaries and often starting conflicts. But you're reading this book so that you can make your work life more effective, so lean in and focus on this next paragraph.

As we've discussed, students raised in poverty typically experience both acute and chronic stress at higher levels than middle- and upper-class learners (Evans & Schamberg, 2009). In addition, those from lower-socioeconomic statuses typically have fewer coping skills and face more stressors, longer-lasting stressors, and more severe, intense stressors (Evans, 2004). There are only two primary behavioral responses to chronic stressors: (1) hypervigilance (high level of alertness, being edgy and angry) or (2) learned helplessness (detached and demotivated; Maier & Watkins, 2005). Have you seen students in either of those two states?

This means you often have edgy, stressed students showing up at school. Now, let's tie this to our chapter title. A student's perception of control over stress is a potent coping mechanism that may convey resilience because feeling more in control lowers stress (Yehuda, Flory, Southwick, & Charney, 2006). That's why control and choice are key.

Choice and control are critical because your students need them both, but they rarely get them. Remove these from a school setting, and you will lose your students. Stress and control are at opposite ends of the spectrum. But feeling more in control lowers stress (Yehuda et al., 2006). It's a breath of fresh air. That's why your students crave more control at school; they are rarely getting it at home. Helping your students feel control over a stressor reduces the behavioral and neurochemical consequences of future uncontrollable stressors (like threats from their neighborhood, peers, or home; Amat, Paul, Zarza, Watkins, & Maier, 2006; Baratta et al., 2009). This phenomenon is called *behavioral immunization*, meaning you can actively reshape your students' stress circuitry. For example, giving students a mildly stressful event (like speaking in front of peers) can immunize the student, thereby strengthening resistance to subsequent stressors. Such a boost to a student's immunological memory can increase stress resilience. You must ask yourself every day, "How do I empower my students with a balance of stress and control so they feel alive and ready to take on tough academic and social challenges?" This is where relevance comes in. When students feel invested in what they're learning, if they understand how it applies to their lives (or you remind them of their dreams and related goals you mapped out with them), they're experiencing increased control.

When control increases, a sense of personal efficacy also increases. Another study shows that students who perceive that their classrooms accept and encourage their autonomy in the first few weeks increase their engagement throughout the course, rather than withdraw from it (Hafen et al., 2012).

I cannot be any blunter: help your students gain more control over their daily lives in your class. *Perceived control* (the belief that your actions can actually make a difference in your life) typically develops throughout young adulthood. In school, task performance increases when students find value and have interest in the content (O'Keefe & Linnenbrink-Garcia, 2014). Learning to give away control to your students will help keep you from struggling with students from poverty. Keep asking yourself, "How can I engage students more, give them more control, and help them develop leadership and autonomy?"

One salient way we can define all learning at school is through the *choice filter*. Students learn either by choice or compliance—either it's the student's idea (he or she chose it) or it was someone else's (a teacher's, parent's, friend's, or so on). The brain saves choice learning pretty well, because it's more likely to be behaviorally relevant, but not compliance learning. If the brain chooses to learn something, it finds it more relevant. See figure 5.1.

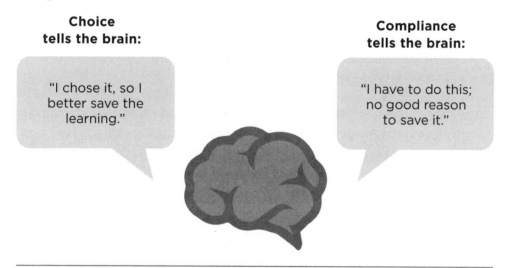

Choice tells the brain:

"I chose it, so I better save the learning."

Compliance tells the brain:

"I have to do this; no good reason to save it."

Figure 5.1: Choice versus compliance.

Granting students choices and control over the content and when they study it can enhance long-term memory (Murty, DuBrow, & Davachi, 2015; Voss, Gonsalves, Federmeier, Tranel, & Cohen, 2011). (See chapter 12, page 103, for more on memory.) This is powerful research; when students choose, they are more likely to form strong memories.

This also tells us that gimmick-free choices are important (such as allowing them to choose any topic to write about). Your students can tell instantly when teachers use bribes, punishments, or rewards to coerce them. Initially, a student's response might be,

"How do I play the game to avoid pain or gain pleasure?" Ultimately, it is the strength of your relationship with students that will help with their decision making ("That's not a good choice, but I like her, so I'll roll with it"). In the short term, some reward-based strategies might work, but be cautious about assuming all students like rewards. You run the risk of students saying, "I didn't *really* have a choice. I was conned." They will always correlate rewards, in the long haul, with *loss of control*. There is no real choice if students cannot make a free, uncoerced decision about the learning. Allow students to choose a topic to learn, the type of presentation (such as PowerPoint, lecture, or a skit), and the week in which to present it. Stop using concrete rewards (like points for prizes or parties), and start with what matters most to students: a feeling of control, choice, and meaning (relevance). For example, selecting a student's mathematics or science project to appear in a fair is both relevant and status building. It is how we feel that is most important to us.

Students feel more in charge of their lives when they get to choose. A secondary mathematics teacher gave his students one hundred problems to start a semester (Soloveichik, 1979). He also gave them choices about *when* to do the problems and *whether* to do the problems. Most students completed all of them each semester (Soloveichik, 1979). Students are more likely to love mathematics when they understand how to do the problems, when it is a social activity, and when they get choices.

It's critical to "sell the choice" by drawing attention to it and the benefits of having it because otherwise, they won't see it or appreciate it. Your goal is to make the choice sound good so that students are excited about being able to choose. For example, say something like, "Hey, we are about to do something, but first, I have an idea. How many of you would like to *have a choice* on whether you work alone or with a partner so you can do things your way? (*Hands go up.*) Great, I thought so. How many would rather choose from among three project ideas instead of me assigning one to you? This time, you do get a choice, so go ahead and get started."

When students share their choices, honor them. Never diminish students' choices. If a student makes a poor choice, say, "I would never have guessed that you would choose that. Tell me more about your decision. How did you come up with it?" This shows that you care. On a practical note, remember to be mindful of your voice volume and tonality. Never yell at students or embarrass them in front of their peers. Certainly avoid sarcasm and threats to your students, since both may trigger the stress response.

Figure 5.2 offers strategies for control, choice, and relevancy. The following sections describe these in more detail. Then, we'll take a look at control, choice, and relevancy in action in a real classroom.

Quick Writes

Some teachers struggle to come up with choices all day. One of the simplest strategies is also one of the most powerful: writing. Through writing, students have a chance to

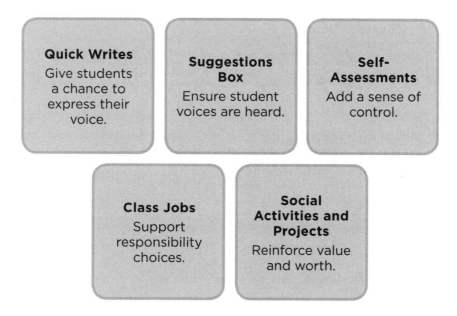

Figure 5.2: Strategies for control, choice, and relevancy.

express their voice. It also builds vocabulary, formalizes thoughts, and organizes ideas. It's a concrete takeaway to show parents or store at home. These all contribute to a more positive mindset because students feel more in control so their stress goes down. Quick writes allow students to use choice for a short time. They choose their own words and can solve a problem. Three groups of students wrote about either a positive or negative emotional event for fifteen minutes over three days (Lyubomirsky et al., 2006). At the end, which do you think felt better, emotionally?

If you predicted it was those who analyzed a negative event, you're correct! Students who wrote about and analyzed negative experiences actually improved their well-being. Those who both wrote about and analyzed their happiest moments reduced their well-being relative to those who replayed these moments only (Lyubomirsky et al., 2006). The takeaway is that it's better to enjoy the good moments (replay without analyzing) and analyze the bad moments for a better mood. This is a simple but powerful tool that can help students influence their own attitudes.

Suggestions Box

A suggestions box is another form of choice; give students the right to communicate their needs, voice an opinion, or make requests. Encourage this input before class, during class, in notes you write, and during one-on-one time. Ask, "What do you think?" or "How do you feel about this?" Then, ask, "How could you let others know what you care about?"

Self-Assessments

Involve students in assessments. Give students access to the scores and the potential follow-up strategies to fix any problems. Students can discuss with their teacher the 3Ms. They are: (1) What is my milestone? (Where am I right now or what score did I get?), (2) What is my mission? (How can I get 100 percent on the next quiz or test?), and (3) What is my method to get there? (What's my plan to fulfill mission?). When your students can effectively self-assess, they feel an important sense of control over their lives.

Class Jobs

Grant autonomy through class jobs. Remind students weekly that they always have a choice in life; they are their own bus drivers.

- Ensure students have key roles in class. These could include stretch or energizer leader (fitness trainer), announcement maker (news anchor), team leader (group manager), summarizer (writer or reporter), logistics manager, and others.

- Give overt choices about when students can accomplish a task, with whom they will do it, which format the work will be done on, and what the deliverable will be. Just don't make any two of those choice variables at the same time.

Social Activities and Projects

There are two main types of social activities: those inside or outside of class. In-class activities include the use of problem-based learning, small-group presentations, and teamwork on segments from a text, lesson plan, or class-related website. Each requires and fosters the use of positive social skills. Outside-of-class projects include mentoring other students, participating in school-culture projects (banners, gardens, or events), or doing community work (spending time with senior citizens, people with disabilities, or the homeless). The beauty of outside-of-class activities is that students make choices, use some control over their work, and sculpt it for greater relevancy.

Control, Choice, and Relevancy in Action

Here's what one successful high school mathematics teacher at a high-poverty school does to give his students a sense of choice, control, and relevancy (Irish, 2012). First, he introduces *gutsy goals*—that is, big, long-term goals—by posting the mathematics score that students need on the college entrance exam to be eligible for a scholarship. Second, to track the progress of his mathematics classes, he posts the nearby competitor school's scores. Using his class's test scores, he scores students at the advanced, mastery, basic, approaching basic, and unsatisfactory levels. He then shares the competitor's scores.

He has taught students how to evaluate their scores and set actionable goals for the next test. The students have *chosen* to keep track of their own scores. When it's time for students to share, he hears, "I got basic, but I want mastery next time. I need to ask more questions in class" or "I got advanced on the bowl game (recent quiz), but my partner did worse. I need to make sure I'm helping him when we are doing class activities." This activity shifts ownership of learning from the teacher to the students. Students can feel both autonomy and freedom to make choices. Notice how this sense of autonomy he has fostered in his students drives their effort and growth. This is what supporting choice, control, and relevancy is all about.

Quick Consolidation

You saw two primary behavior responses to chronic stressors: (1) hypervigilance (such as alertness, edginess, or anger) and (2) learned helplessness (detachment and demotivation). You can either get frustrated with students' behavior or take action to help them and make your own workplace a positive environment. Choice, control, and relevancy are connected. Give your students relevant choices and help them develop autonomy over their daily experiences. Most typical middle- and upper-class students will get tastes of choice, control, and relevancy at home. But students raised in poverty typically experience fewer of these, which can generate helplessness and anger. The solution is to be mindful of these success factors. These invisible factors are not typically in your standards or lesson plans. But they should be. Can you start this process? When can you begin?

CHAPTER 6

CHANGE THE EMOTIONAL SET POINT

Going back hundreds of years, two of the biggest mistaken beliefs include, "The Earth is flat" and "Brains can't change." Today, we know better. The Earth is round, and brains can change. In fact, the so-called *set point* for weight management (feeling full) can be changed, as well as your tolerance for pain (the *ouch* tolerance), your happiness (joy), and your stress level. The *emotional set point* signifies a person's most common emotional state. For some, it is frustration and anger. For others, it is calmness and joy. The good news is teachers can alter a student's emotional set point.

What's the relevance of this? We now know that we can help students who were considered incorrigible, lazy, or aggressive. It just takes the right mindset and skill set. When you do this, you are a richer teacher. The problem is most people don't have the mindset or know how to change the set points, so their usual (and false) conclusion is, "Maybe it is just not possible to change these students." This conclusion is a huge mistake for two reasons. First, the teacher is robbed of the joy of transforming a student into a healthy adult who will find work, meaning, and success. Second, the student (whom the teacher has given up on) becomes relegated to a life absent of the joys of transformation, change, and meaning.

Evidence Behind the Emotional Set Point

The majority of school-age students living in poverty is exposed to multiple chronic stressors including violence, family turmoil, separation from family members, and substandard living environments (Evans & Kim, 2012). Students are also more sensitive to social stress (Sripada, Swain, Evans, Welsh, & Liberzon, 2014).

The human brain adapts to the chronic stress by creating a new normal set point. While it is a coping tool, this also sets up the brain for problems. Examples of new set points for stress are hypervigilance (aggressive, in-your-face behavior) and hyporesponsiveness (learned helplessness). But you can help change this rewired brain if you know how to do it. It is all about the emotions.

Emotions run our brains, particularly those of school-age students. Our behaviors rely on connections between the amygdala and prefrontal cortex. Classroom behaviors that connect with emotions include learning (Delgado, Nearing, LeDoux, & Phelps, 2008; Milad et al., 2007) and regulation (Goldin, McRae, Ramel, & Gross, 2008; Lieberman et al., 2007). These are both critical for success because coping well requires interplay between cognition and emotions. Coping well reduces reactivity to stress in school, which can lead to academic success (Adler, Conklin, & Strunk, 2013).

The good news is that this set point for happiness is adjustable, and changing it is transformative for students and you too. Long-running research surveys show that personal and economic choices matter more for happiness than genes (Headey, Muffels, & Wagner, 2010). You can change your students' happiness set point but only if you know how to do it. The key is consistency rather than holding a random event per week or month. See figure 6.1.

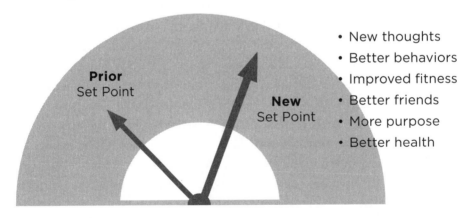

Figure 6.1: Change students' happiness set point.

Why are emotions so important in the classroom? The answer may surprise you. When people are grumpy, they occasionally make poor decisions. When depression, anger, or irritation is one's semi-permanent life state, he or she may often make poor decisions.

When you teach students to make better choices, and foster a better emotional climate, the student's emotional set point changes. This is not simple to do, but it is well worth it. Improved emotions can foster better decisions, and better decisions can foster improved emotions.

When students succeed and feel good at school, their daily happiness improves. But it turns out that the *type* of happiness they're feeling is what matters (Catalino & Fredrickson, 2011). There are three types of happiness, and each has a very different effect on your students, both at a practical level and even at a genetic level (Catalino & Fredrickson, 2011).

1. **Spontaneous happiness:** The enjoyment to be found in the moment (ice cream, a surprise of a beautiful flower opening up, a smile, a gift, a kiss, or sunset)

2. **Hedonic happiness:** The pursuit of pleasure for its own sake (being addicted to video games, online shopping, unhealthy foods, gambling, excess TV, or hoarding)

3. **Eudaimonic happiness:** The joyful satisfaction of long-term pursuit of worthwhile goals (becoming part of an athletic team that has a good season, learning a tough new skill, building something relevant, or leading an interesting project)

See figure 6.2. You might think, "Happy is happy. It's just a matter of how mild or intense." But there's more to it than that.

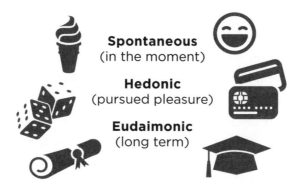

Figure 6.2: Three types of happiness.

To understand how and why these tie into teaching, it's important to know how your brain responds differently to each of the three happiness types.

The first type of happiness is spontaneous joy as from a surprise (running into a good friend, eating a meal that turned out better than expected, seeing or smelling a beautiful flower, or watching your hapless team win at the last second). The primary distinction here is that the joy is unplanned and unpursued. In the classroom, it could happen when a teacher surprises her students with a joke, a fun energizer, a funny story, or an early departure. The brain's response is the release of dopamine, the neurotransmitter of pleasure.

Hedonic happiness is distinguished by two qualities: (1) it is a planned pursuit, and (2) the person seeks pleasure as the outcome. This is known as a hedonic experience, which is often, but not always, part of our everyday lives. You may know people who have dangerous hobbies such as gambling, unrestrained cravings for fatty or sweet foods, or alcohol addiction, or even just spend excessive time on the Internet, shop compulsively, or constantly gossip about peers. This hedonic pleasure has some problems. In the classroom, you might reinforce hedonic happiness with the chronic use of material rewards such as bribes of sweets and treats or points redeemable for more rewards.

Again, the primary distinction here is that people plan and look forward to a predictable outcome from the experience. Do you reward yourself with food when something good happens? Do you promise good things to your students if they behave right? That's a likely mistake (Disabato, Goodman, Kashdan, Short, & Jarden, 2015). The brain's response to a prediction of reward is the release of dopamine, the neurotransmitter of pleasure (Sharot, Shiner, Brown, Fan, & Dolan, 2009). But after several times, the brain habituates to the reward, meaning that once the reward happens, it releases no dopamine. The pleasure response diminishes, and the rewarded behavior becomes a letdown. This type of happiness becomes harder and harder to achieve. This is one reason why drugs are so addictive.

Humans can become addicted to anything: drugs, sex, sugar, fats, cars, shopping, and crime. Addiction is a biological state that drives the organism *with a compulsive engagement* to receive the rewarding stimuli, despite adverse consequences and a loss of control over the behavior. In the classroom, students can become driven to get a teacher's reward, in spite of it being bad for the student.

The third type of happiness is eudaimonic (pronounced *you-day-monic*). Eudaimonic happiness leads directly to meaningful goals—just as graduating (see the graduation mindset on page 121). Make it your goal to foster an emotionally positive classroom climate. Happier students work harder and are far more enjoyable to teach. This happy state comes not from consuming but from producing something. It's the byproduct of a sustained effort in working toward something bigger than you: seeking purposeful and meaningful goals. It's the pursuit of big goals and mastery learning. This type of joy actually fuels the drive to achieve and helps the body thrive too. In fact, it's even associated with increased gray matter in the brain (Lewis, Kanai, Rees, & Bates, 2014). While there are some anatomical exceptions and limitations, increases in gray matter (brain mass) and white matter (myelin coating on connecting tissue between cells known as axons) are associated with a higher brain functioning. In other words, it is fabulous!

Those who found happiness by pursuing the greater good (long-term, eudaimonic, purposeful goals) had a lower level of inflammatory gene expression and strong antiviral and antibody gene expression (Algoe & Fredrickson, 2011). This is a dramatically healthier profile, and the benefits include better school attendance for the secondary students in the study. These individuals are more likely to stay healthy, avoid drugs, and exhibit greater resilience (Cohn, Fredrickson, Brown, Mikels, & Conway, 2009). Wouldn't you wish these benefits for your students?

How to Change Students' Emotional Set Points

There are two ways to change students' emotional set points: intensity (like trauma, obviously not a good idea) or relevant duration (language learning). In your classroom, this means you'll be doing relevant things over time. You can use meaningful projects, focus on the end product, tie feedback to quality, and reinforce what is working. For example, K–12 students who work hard for long-term goals (like high school graduation) may find meaning and joy in the process. Additionally, strong social ties, the capacity to derive meaning, and personal growth are common correlations for eudaimonic state (Ryff, 2014).

Use Meaningful Projects

Assign work projects that last longer than just a week or two. It turns out that adolescents (grades 6–12) who focus over a semester or a year on eudaimonic (long-term) pleasures have less risk of depression (Telzer, Fuligni, Lieberman, & Galván, 2014). Ideas for you include relevant project-based learning, service work, or team assignments with collaboration over weeks and months. When you help your students do meaningful, relevant projects (versus only short worksheets), they have a better chance of getting healthier and happier! High-performing teachers do these consistently.

Focus on the End Product

Start an assignment by first focusing on the end product. That means you'll want to get buy-in to the end goal and then strengthen the intensity of the value. Tell students about the benefits, have them draw a picture of how they'll feel, ask them to share the benefits with a neighbor, and post up a colorful picture of students succeeding at the project. Next, move on to concentrate on the process. That is, the hook to involve students may be a gutsy goal, and it also helps with relevancy (see page 45). But once students get into the process, then you can focus on the quality of the work. That's where the satisfaction is.

Tie Feedback to Quality

Students need to learn what great work looks like. They also need to see that their teachers care about the quality of their work, not how fast they can get it done. Show great quality sample student work to your students so they know what you want. Circulate the examples and post them in the class. This ties their emotional satisfaction to a more lasting event, product, or service.

Reinforce What Is Working

Ensure that you keep students in the game with simple reinforcers. These include smiles, affirmations, celebrations, written feedback, team bragging, shared individual success, partner comments, personal interactions, and acknowledgments of quality work. This approach echoes what researchers know: positive reinforcement works better than negative reinforcement (Nelson, Demers, & Christ, 2014).

The eudaimonic state of happiness is an everyday mood-generating state that works magic in your school. Students will attend class more when they are sick less often. They try harder and succeed more often in school. This cycles positive energy and hope back to the teachers, who in turn feel affirmed and rewarded. This powerful process is invisible yet powerful (Algoe & Fredrickson, 2011).

Quick Consolidation

There are several types of happiness. The serendipity of a simple, surprising happy moment is, of course, still a great idea. But the pursuit of pleasure for pleasure's sake is not very good for our well-being. The long-term pursuit of meaningful goals is actually more than invigorating; it's healthier and more positive than short-term pleasure seeking.

This is why tough projects and goals can work miracles with your students. If you reflected on each of these earlier, you have already started the process for a high-achieving classroom. These create a highly positive classroom climate. Your students will love coming to school when you sustain these in your work. How can you get started on these strategies?

CHAPTER 7

LOCK IN THE POSITIVITY MINDSET

How do you get students to develop a rock-solid positive attitude? Every highly successful teacher has to find his or her own way. One special education teacher at the elementary level in the Midwest is typically the last resort for her students. Josalyn Tresvant (The New Teacher Project, 2013) teaches fifth graders in a high-poverty school in Memphis, Tennessee. Everything she does is purposeful and designed to ensure that her students will thrive. To establish relevance, she brings her prior banking experience to the classroom, showing students why they need to learn mathematics, reading, and writing.

She starts with developing a new identity for her students. She addresses them as *scholars* and cultivates a no-excuses attitude in her class. She empowers her students to take responsibility for how they're doing in several ways. She teaches them to start with themselves, not blame others. Her students become proficient in technology, and she makes students' data available to them so they can see how they're doing. She encourages students to develop a positive attitude through accountability, empowerment, and responsibility. She debriefs students on their progress to shape their ongoing narratives and develop their identities.

Her students learn about attitudes in many ways during class. She introduces her vision, the big goal. To help reach it, she teaches students to reflect on their wins (classroom successes) and challenges (the current problem to overcome). This helps her students link actions to goals using attribution thinking: "When I do this, I get that." As with other high performers, she "walks the talk" and models what she teaches. For example, she videotapes her classes and reviews her own work for mistakes or lost opportunities.

This teacher is a light that shines every day with the positivity mindset. She continually asks herself, "In what ways can I develop unbridled hope and optimism and still keep my students grounded in reality?" These positive attitudes are not only teachable, but countless teachers have already proven to do an amazing job of teaching them. The preceding chapters have shown you how to develop them in your students.

Change the Narrative, Change Your Teaching

The narrative is the explanatory description of what is happening in your class. It includes both your and your students' lives. You know you have a choice in life, and you know that you can change your work (and personal) life by changing your narrative. Are you willing to change your narrative about success and failures? If so, you can script out a new (and better) ending.

In the classroom it means you can raise student achievement (even while putting out the same effort as before) if you first choose to change your beliefs, attitudes, and mindsets that form the story. Your narrative is one of the single strongest predictors of how your life unfolds. The narrative is the ongoing story. When you become fully convinced that you have a choice in life and don't have to repeat the past, you realize that you can change your life story. How can you do it?

In a way, you are writing a novel with your life. You choose where to work, your life partners, and your friends. At work, you choose your words, you influence each student interaction, and you make decisions. You don't always choose what happens to you, but you do choose how you respond to what happens to you. You choose to color your day with either emotions of positive energy, humility, grace, and confidence, or to fill the day with complaints. Yes, you are choreographing your life. If it were a novel, would it end well? What mindset narrative do you have? See figure 7.1.

You, as the teacher, are leading students to build a positive narrative. Josalyn didn't wake up in the morning and win a lottery. She made choices that changed lives, again and again. Remember, you don't always get to choose what happens to you, but you can choose how you respond to what happens to you. She doesn't get to choose who her students are in class. But she makes every day great for them. When you wake up each morning to go to work, you can resolve to help your students succeed by using the success tools of hope and optimism. In short, never ever let a chance to foster positivity go to waste. You want to use every opportunity you can to make your class awesome and help your students on the path to graduation.

You Are Your Mindset: Which Is Yours?

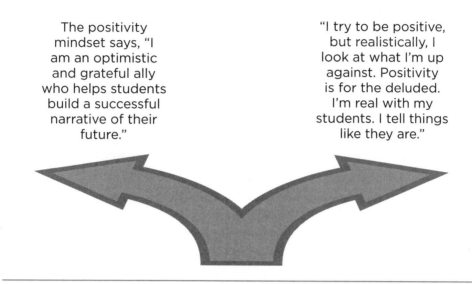

The positivity mindset says, "I am an optimistic and grateful ally who helps students build a successful narrative of their future."

"I try to be positive, but realistically, I look at what I'm up against. Positivity is for the deluded. I'm real with my students. I tell things like they are."

Figure 7.1: You are your mindset—the positivity mindset.

Fill in the following blanks with your name and a strategy from this mindset. Repeat the phrase daily until it's automatic.

"I, _____, am committing to developing the positivity mindset with my students every single day. I will begin with one of the strategies mentioned, which is _____. I will continue this until I have mastery and it's automatic. At that point, I'll learn something new to foster student success."

Reflection and Decision

All meaningful and lasting change starts with a mirror. Self-reflect first. I thought I was positive until I met people who were *really* positive. Is this possibly true for you? The positivity mindset is for every teacher. Once you have it, sharing with students and instilling it daily will become second nature. What is more important to you: helping your students become more positive, or feeling comfortable with the old negative mindset?

The most important thing I've learned about life is this: you always have a choice—even when you think you don't. When your pay freezes for another year, the state adopts a new set of curriculum standards, you disagree with leadership at school, and you get students who are not prepared or ready for your grade level or subject, you still have a choice. You could complain about how bad things are and do nothing about it. But that's not productive.

At the end of the day (or month, or year, or even career), you're no better off being a complainer. You are more likely to become bitter and miserable. Keep this at the front of your brain: you always have a choice. If you aren't happy where you are, find a different job in education, move overseas and teach in an international school, or switch career paths and do something entirely different. Do what you ask your students to do: focus on optimism and hope, remember your strengths, be grateful, perform acts of kindness, and take responsibility for how you react to what happens to you. You can sculpt your life to be more awesome, or you can feel like a victim, swimming away from sharks for the rest of your life. It's your choice.

In other words, pause and ask a big question: "How do I want to invest the rest of my career?" Are you going to dismiss the hard scientific research on the power of positivity, claiming that it's not your thing, or are you going to make positivity your mindset, starting today? Your decision to develop a positivity mindset in yourself and students includes (1) creating a new narrative about your students and yourself, (2) choosing a positivity strategy to develop with a fierce urgency, and (3) creating a support process to ensure successful implementation. That support process may include talking with colleagues, writing notes to yourself, and crafting lesson plans with your new strategies and narratives. This is the truth about what it takes to succeed in this tough, gritty profession. You can do this.

Quick Consolidation

The positivity mindset influences many areas of teaching. You get opportunities to develop and foster positivity through optimism and hope; positive attitudes; choice, control, and relevancy; and the emotional set point. The hard work is in choosing, over and over, to do the work. The work itself is just work—you already do that every day. You're invited to do the same amount of work you already do but just a little differently. Once you begin supporting the positivity mindset, you'll be growing students emotionally every day. Next up, let's build your students cognitively.

PART TWO

WHY THE ENRICHMENT MINDSET?

CHAPTER 8

SECRETS OF THE ENRICHMENT MINDSET

Like many teachers at the beginning of the school year, I used to notice myself making those instant judgments about my students as they arrived. Today, in light of the new research on teacher beliefs and mindsets, I am embarrassed to admit thinking things like, "I'll bet she will do really well" or "He probably won't do that well." Even though I thought of myself as positive and encouraging to my students, in retrospect, I would bet that students could sense my small doubts. In fact, they were hearing, "My teacher doesn't like me or believe in me."

Your first response may be, "It's only human to think that way." Although you might be right, if your goal is to maximize every student's potential, you just dropped the ball. A teacher who thinks this is not supporting the enrichment mindset. While those with the growth mindset (Dweck, 2008) say, "We can all grow," the enrichment mindset broadens the concept to "We can all grow above and beyond what we thought was possible."

The question I should have asked was: "If I actually buy that all students can learn, why would I put *any* mental limit on a student?" The answer is important. When I thought about *some* students having a cognitive limitation, the person I was really thinking about was myself.

Yes, it's true. When a teacher, anywhere, talks about a student's cognitive limitations, he or she is commonly talking about his or her own limitations. Teachers with this thinking are talking about their own inability to reach and teach students in ways that propel them forward. If teachers say that they'll never be able to improve the IQ of a student with learning delays, that is their own personal experience and history of frustrations. Students with learning delays are typically behind grade level in speech, language, memory, and writing skills. But on a larger scale, IQ in learning-delayed students often improves with the right strategies (Duyme, Dumaret, & Tomkiewicz, 1999).

The Enrichment Mindset

The following chapters are all about building the enrichment mindset. To grasp the mindset, we can contrast it with the opposite mindsets—*fixed*—of teachers who struggle with growing the capacity of students. As a reminder, the fixed mindset suggests that personal characteristics are unchangeable—you either have them (IQ, talent, or a knack), or you don't. You may have heard a teacher say one or more of the following statements, or something similar.

- "If they haven't learned how to do this by now, they'll never learn it."
- "These students have failed so much before, they already know they can't do it."
- "Some students get it and others don't. I cover the content. If they're ready, they'll learn it."
- "You can see it in their eyes. Some students have just given up."
- "He tried hard, but bless his heart. It's not going to happen."

That thinking is dead wrong. As noted, Stanford University professor Carol Dweck is a pioneering researcher on motivation and, specifically, mindsets. Surprisingly, she did not begin by studying success. Instead, she studied failures. To make sense of this mindset, Dweck (2008) made key distinctions among a range of responses that all of us could potentially have linked to any particular failure. To Dweck, failure was not the problem; it is how we handle our failures. It turns out that *after you fail* is when we see your character. The enrichment mindset takes the growth mindset further. In contrast, the enrichment mindset sounds more like the following statements from teachers.

- "I will learn and grow from my mistakes. Mistakes are feedback that helps me get better."
- "My setback tells me to try something different next time. A new strategy might change things."
- "I will learn from criticism and never try to avoid it."
- "I will persist until I succeed. More effort or a different strategy is justified."
- "If I keep at this, I know I'll get it."
- "I might not be a genius, but I'll work harder than the next person."

The bottom line is that your thoughts and beliefs do matter. The belief changes the decision you make, which in turn changes your behaviors. Behaviors over time become habits, and those habits become your character. The enrichment mindset says, "I know brains can change. I can grow and change myself first. Then, I can build powerful cognitive skills in my students."

> The enrichment mindset says, "I know brains can change. I can grow and change myself first. Then, I can build powerful cognitive skills in my students."

The enrichment mindset is critical. In short, it is often our mindsets and our internal narratives about why we were failing that shape our future. All of us fail at some point. The question to ask yourself is, "How do I respond to failure, both personally and as a teacher?" Remember, the enrichment mindset broadens the growth mindset.

A Hard Look at the Evidence

Dweck's (2008) work predicted that people's results came about not because they failed, but because of their beliefs about *why* they failed. Understanding failure is critical because every one of us will fail in life.

When we attribute our failures to the faults of others or a lack of our own ability, circumstances, IQ, genes, or talent, we get discouraged. If we label our failures as normal, everyday setbacks, and we tie them to temporary (and changeable) variables, setbacks are likely to fuel us. Those variables are:

- Lack of effort
- A poor attitude
- Inappropriate strategy
- Lack of tools
- Insufficient experience

Failure at some point is certain, but it is *how* teachers and students respond to failure that matters. IQ, talent, and capacity are not fixed and can be developed. Students should choose to learn from mistakes, grow, and become better. They have control over their brains, effort, strategies, and attitude, and can improve all of these.

Here's an example of how much the human brain can change. Researcher Harold Skeels (1966) had a different mindset than most. Although his research is several decades old, it has a powerful impact on how we see enrichment. He wondered if the devastating results from suboptimal upbringings in first graders could be reversible. He found a group of thirteen children designated by the orphanage assessment officer as unsuitable for adoption based on cognitive levels. These students were then transferred to, and lodged in, an institution specifically for those with developmental disabilities. Skeels provided daily enriched learning and positive social conditions for these students. His enrichment started with close, positive, caring relationships, and he used social games through the day. He also carefully documented an alternative control group of orphans at the same institution who were deemed suitable for adoption. This group was matched as closely as possible to the experiment's orphans.

The experiment continued for three years, with a follow-up two years later. After five years total, his experimental enrichment group had an average *gain* of almost twenty-nine IQ points, while the control group had a *loss* of about twenty-six points (Skeels, 1966). See figure 8.1. Stop and think: do you still think brains cannot change? Do you still think IQ is fixed for life? If so, it's time to shift your mindset; anything is possible.

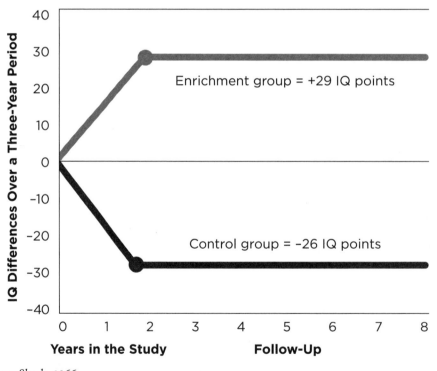

Source: Skeels, 1966.

Figure 8.1: Enrichment changes IQ.

This trend continued five years later. The thirty-year follow-up for the experimental group revealed that grade 12 (high school graduation) was the median completed grade versus grade 2.75 (about third grade) for the control group who stayed in the orphanage (Skeels, 1996). Finally, to emphasize the possible far-reaching implications, the twenty-eight children from the parents of the experimental group who became parents (the next generation) had a mean IQ from school records of 104. This shows the difference enrichment made on the students' lives. Remember this study in your everyday work: your students' brains can change. Are you willing to give this a try?

You see, it's limiting when a teacher says, "You can't do that!" To be more truthful, a teacher might say, "I wish I knew how to help this student. She deserves better." That statement is honest, but most people use the coping tool to justify or blame others ("It's the student's fault"), so they can sleep at night. But you and I now know better. This is a challenge, but I suspect you are up for it. Consider the conversation in figure 8.2.

Figure 8.2: Place no limits on students.

Let me rephrase what you just read. You may have heard a teacher saying, "Kevin's just not going to get good at mathematics" or "Sheron has a tough time with writing; it's just not her thing." The teacher is *really* saying, "I don't know how to help Kevin or Sheron do better, so I'll speak as if no one could ever help him or her succeed." You can help them succeed, and I'll show you how.

Just in case you're still wondering if students' brains can change, let's review more scientific research on whether the brain is fixed or malleable, if a growth mindset is teachable, how to respond when students struggle, and the cognitive differences of students from poverty.

Is the Brain Fixed or Malleable?

Science has refuted most notions of a fixed brain. We know, for example, that the human brain grows new brain cells every day (Eriksson et al., 1998). Just as important, research shows that variables regulate this process, some of which we have control over, such as exercise (Pereira et al., 2007). Think about that for a moment. Your brain, which typically might produce one thousand new brain cells every day, could actually produce more or less than that depending on how you live your life. You are actively sculpting each student's brain in class every day!

We know that the cells make new connections from school experiences (Berns, Blaine, Prietula, & Pye, 2013). Research has shown that IQ can change (Duyme et al., 1999; Nesbitt, 2009). Nutrition can improve IQ (Schoenthaler, Bier, Young, Nichols, & Jansenns, 2000). Simply reading a novel for thirty minutes a day for nine consecutive days creates more brain connections (Berns et al., 2013). Teaching reasoning changes the brain (Mackey, Whitaker, & Bunge, 2012). You can boost fluid intelligence—logical thinking—with repetitive training (Au et al., 2015).

We also know that school experiences with above-average teachers can raise student achievement in mathematics by as much as two standard deviations (Ferguson, 1998). Many high-poverty schools graduate 95 percent and more of seniors, so the excuses for failure are getting thinner by the day (Carter, 2001; Parrett & Budge, 2012).

Can We Teach the Enrichment Mindset?

Dweck's (2008) research on the growth mindset supports the notion that our mindset after and before we fail predicts our future results. How does the research support these claims?

Mindset researchers tested a specific cognitive enhancement for preschool-age children (Segretin et al., 2014). They formed two groups, the experimental and the control group. They gave the experimental group a four-month growth mindset program. The preK students were told, "Your brain can change. Your brain can change. You can change and grow. Your attitude, effort, and strategies will determine your eventual success." In the end, the experimental group not only outperformed the control group but sustained its positive results for years (Segretin et al., 2014). Dweck (2008) discovered that when presented with a sliding scale of fixed to growth mindsets, we are likely to fall on a continuum when exposed to various scenarios. See figure 8.3 for some examples of two extreme ends of the mindset continuum.

Fixed	How each mindset responds to:	Growth
Avoids them	⇦ Challenges ⇨	Embraces them
Gives up easily	⇦ Obstacles ⇨	Persists
Sees it as not justified	⇦ Effort ⇨	Sees it as a must
Dismisses it	⇦ Criticism ⇨	Uses it
Feels threatened	⇦ Others' success ⇨	Feels inspired

Figure 8.3: Fixed versus growth mindsets.

Next, research with K–5 children using computer games shows that the growth mindset enhances persistence (O'Rourke, Haimovitz, Ballweber, Dweck, & Popović, 2014). And even in the toughest classes (like physics), secondary students with the growth mindset did better than those with a fixed mindset (Flores, Lemons, & McTernan, 2011).

In secondary mathematics classes, students with growth mindset training outperformed those who did not get this training, even two years after the initial exposure (Blackwell, Trzesniewski, & Dweck, 2007). Students' academic performance improves when they are simply exposed to a growth mindset, even when the teaching itself remains the same.

In one study (Jensen, 2014) with ten high-poverty schools (75 percent or more students in poverty), half of the schools were high performing (in the top 25 percent of academic performers in the state) and half were low performing (lowest 25 percent of academic scores in the state). What was the difference in these schools? The students were from high-poverty backgrounds, but the staff at the high-performing schools fostered a better growth mindset, created a strong school culture, and built cognitive capacity.

When students struggle, how do they respond? How do *you* respond? As we have learned, how we deal with failure can support the enrichment mindset, if we first have a growth mindset. See figure 8.4 (page 72).

Fixed Mindsets Versus Growth Mindsets

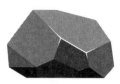   **OR**

- It is all cast in stone.
- I am stuck the way I am.
- I was born this way.
- I likely won't change.
- I am always like this.
- Nothing will change things.

- Nothing is cast in stone.
- I can grow and change.
- DNA is not my destiny.
- I change every day.
- I often make changes.
- I can change many things.

Figure 8.4: Contrast of mindsets.

What Cognitive Differences Do Students From Poverty Have?

As we broaden our definition of mindset, we see the enrichment mindset fits right in. It's imperative to take on the challenge to enrich the following three key areas.

Researchers commonly associate low socioeconomic status with differences in performance on a variety of academic endeavors (Farah et al., 2006; Gottfried, Gottfried, Bathurst, Guerin, & Parramore, 2003; Hackman & Farah, 2009). These differences usually involve three core neurocognitive systems: (1) language, (2) memory, and (3) cognitive control. These cognitive differences occur more among the poor (versus the middle class) and can reduce school performance. A variety of home, neighborhood, and school factors contribute to them. The good news is that strong teaching can moderate all of these differences. The variable here is relationships.

The first of the three core neurocognitive systems is language. Students who experience close relationships with their teachers during their early elementary years have stronger receptive language development (Spilt, Koomen, & Harrison, 2015). Greater vocabulary allows students the option of rewording something. The use of rich language allows us to tactfully avoid conflict, write a paper for school, or empathize with a loved one. But the poor have considerable vocabulary gaps. The huge gap in early language exposure between the poor and nonpoor begins as early as eighteen months (Fernald, Marchman, & Weisleder, 2013). The average poor student starting school has been exposed to ten to twenty million fewer words than his or her more affluent peers (Hart & Risley, 1995). The poor consequently learn language skills more slowly and show delays in letter recognition and phonological awareness. Both of these factors increase the risk of reading difficulties (Aikens & Barbarin, 2008).

The second trait is memory, including both long-term and working memory. (Chapter 12, page 103, explains more about both.) Students from poor families are more likely to have deficient working memory than the nonpoor (Evans & Schamberg, 2009). Working memory is a core cognitive skill, necessary for mathematics, reading, and thinking skills. School-age children from low-socioeconomic households also develop baseline academic skills in working memory far more slowly than students from higher socio-economic groups (Morgan, Farkas, Hillemeier, & Maczuga, 2009).

The third trait is cognitive control. This is the capacity to nimbly switch gears and adjust to new circumstances. In the classroom, this translates to students changing their strategy on a problem if one isn't working. On a macro level, it is about transitions. It is also what helps us survive when there are different rules in different settings. Students can say such-and-such to a classmate, but not to a teacher. We learn that if a friend asks if we like her new jeans, and we don't, we can shift to the rules of social harmony and avoid hurting her feelings. These are core life skills, and without them, life is much more difficult. Poor students struggle more than nonpoor students with cognitive control (Hackman & Farah, 2009).

This means that unless you teach them the growth mindset and skills for how to learn, you have just reduced their chances of success. Helping students with metacognitive skills improves motivation, learning, and future learning. Researchers introduced a six-hour training session with middle-school students, teaching them the process skills of planning, monitoring, and evaluating. When researchers later compared their results to those of a control group, the students who learned metacognitive strategies performed better on tests and had higher levels of motivation (Zepeda, Richey, Ronevich, & Nokes-Malach, 2015).

Quick Consolidation

This chapter introduces the enrichment mindset. Although the growth mindset is powerful, it can be broadened to include specific instructional strategies. The single thread through this part is that brains can grow and change and our students can change. We just have to go first.

We all have to examine our mindsets and, when needed, change them. On any single day, you have to choose between sharing a negative story or investing a few minutes of time to help a student with his or her effort, make the smart choice, and succeed. I have visited hundreds of high-poverty schools, and the biggest differences are the educators' mindsets and actions. Your staff members need to take note of Skeels's (1966) mindset, and how he enriched students instead of feeling sorry for them. You must enrich students like crazy to ensure they succeed. When staff members have the negative mindsets about a student being a bad seed or not likely to succeed, the negativity becomes contagious and the student struggles.

This is your opportunity to show your own capacity to grow and help students graduate. If you now recognize your own fixed mindset, your students are not likely to succeed unless you change it. We might call mindset a soft skill, but that's no reason to dismiss it. For some, the difference in mindset is the difference between weak compliance and a huge motivated effort. Alternatively, the mindset may be the difference between staying down and getting back up. The bottom line is that mindset affects each of us differently based on our personal history. Help your students develop the mindset they need to succeed. The next few chapters contain all the strategies you need. You'll never regret your decision.

The following four chapters offer strategies to help you enrich your students. These strategies include the following.

1. Manage the cognitive load.
2. Develop better thinking skills.
3. Enhance study skills and vocabulary.
4. Build better memory.

CHAPTER 9

MANAGE THE COGNITIVE LOAD

Before we get started on enriching your students' brains, you should know what you're up against. When I was an adolescent, I remember sitting in the back of the classroom. My mind usually wandered to questions like, "What will it be like when I go home after school?" I constantly worried about what my abusive stepmother would do. Thoughts that centered on safety were strong and recurring. They seemed to compete with, or block out, thoughts about the class content. Many of your students may have more than an abusive caregiver; they may be facing the burden of raising a younger brother or sister. They may be facing daily racism from the community. They may be hungry and unable to concentrate or can be wondering where they will sleep that night. A student with this much stress has a serious *cognitive load*.

With the enrichment mindset, we do everything we can to enrich a student's brain. This means you will have to address the student's brain. Cognitive load is the quantity of thoughts one has loaded in his or her brain at any given time. It's difficult for students from poverty to concentrate on homework when they have to think about negative factors to survive (such as having enough food, taking abuse from a parent, or so on). It's like having very slow Internet speed. Students from poverty typically experience even greater cognitive load in learning environments than those in middle-class families (Siegler & Alibali, 2005). Unless you address this, you'll perceive such students as slow learners (a result of being unaware of the student's situation and a lack of response, which lead to ineffective teaching). This means that you'll have students who appear distracted and forgetful and ask questions you just answered a moment ago. Cognitive load issues are critical; check for brain interference. See figure 9.1 (page 76).

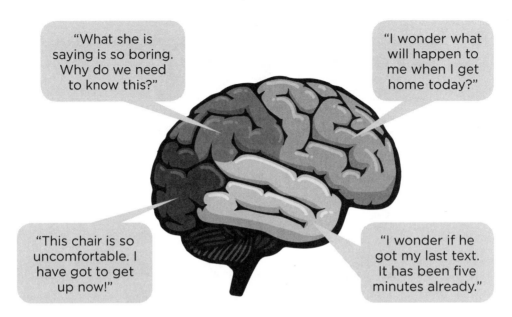

Figure 9.1: Cognitive load.

A student's cognitive ability has an over-the-top effect size on student achievement of 1.04 (Hattie, 2009). But students carrying a heavy cognitive load can't achieve great things when they are mentally consumed with survival. Cognitive load issues happen to everyone, especially students from higher-risk homes (Evans & English, 2002). Your brain's working memory, a sort of mental sketchbook, only has so much space. The cognitive load can be brutal.

Running late for work, your car making weird sounds, and almost being out of gas can become all you think about. If a family member is in the hospital for emergency surgery, it can consume your cognitive bandwidth. To find out the constraints that a cognitive load puts on the brain, researchers artificially induced poverty-like financial worries in middle-class participants with a simulation. When tested before and after, those in the simulation lost up to an equivalent of thirteen IQ points from the cognitive stress (Shah, Mullainathan, & Shafir, 2012). That's because when you want students to think about academics, their brains are already busy processing hour-by-hour survival scenarios. No, your students are not slow or low achieving. Their brains are just occupied.

To solve this critical problem, let's first focus on high-performing teachers. How do they deal with this issue? They start by meeting a basic need in order to reduce their stress: making the classroom physically and emotionally safe with rich relationships. This means never yelling at or berating students. If you do this, you are, metaphorically, throwing gasoline on a fire. Students get enough negatives at home and often arrive feeling stressed. They don't need anger, hostility, or negative attitudes at school. Be the one who changes their lives.

Second, keep them physically active, which generates glucose for the brain. This helps with cognitive skills such as processing speed and memory (Rauner, Walters, Avery, & Wanser, 2013). Consider the following activities.

- **Clap-boom-clap:** Students pay attention and listen to each clap and participate—"Follow along with me. I clap once, and you repeat. Every time I double clap, you say 'Boom!' That tells me you're ready for something big! Are you ready?"

- **Play my sport:** Students stand in teams. One student shows the moves in his or her favorite sport for thirty seconds. The other students mimic that sport's moves until everyone gets a turn. Then another student gets a chance to mimic his or her sport.

- **Follow the leader:** Line students up. Play the song "Follow the Leader" by Soca Boys. When the song starts, the line leader does an action (such as clap, turn right, or stomp), and the others in line must repeat it.

- **Stand up:** Ask students to think about their goal. Then have them take a slow, deep breath and let the breath out fully. Tell them to clench their fists quickly three times and run in place for ten seconds while saying, "I can do this." Now ask them to take one small step toward their goal.

Third, teach students coping skills to help them learn to survive when things get extra tough. For example, use positive self-talk. "Stand up. Take in a slow, deep breath. Ask yourself what your goal is. Answer the question. Let the breath out fully. Clench fists quickly three times. Run in place for ten seconds. Say, I can do this. Now take one small step toward your goal." Strong teachers help students feel more (not less) control over their lives. They engage students with relevant, consuming, nearly impossible goals. Give students a reason to be in school every day. Finally, teaching cognitive skills for reasoning, deferred gratification, and working memory enriches students' thinking in class. Here are tools you can use to counter the cognitive load on the brain.

Tools to Reduce Cognitive Load Issues

Cognitive load consumes students who worry about how their teacher or peers treat them. The key to offsetting it is to make sure that students know that their feelings are important to you and that you care about them. Many times students will "check out" because new content overwhelms them. Here are simple and powerful tools to help students succeed in demanding, sometimes stressful, content-rich classrooms. See figure 9.2 (page 78). In the following sections, you'll notice that each of these simple tools helps students care more, digest better, or remember longer. The tools are simple to use, and they work.

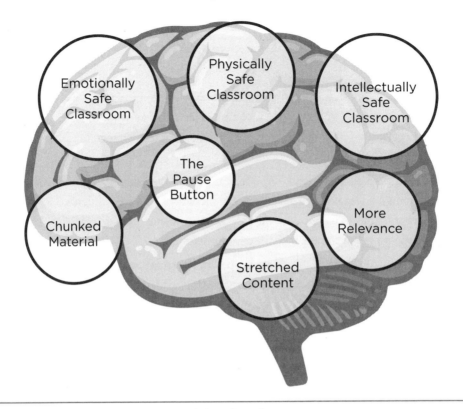

Figure 9.2: Managing cognitive load.

Make the Classroom Emotionally Safe

Make your classroom safe enough for students to be guaranteed they will never be embarrassed, singled out, or yelled at. Ensure that you respond to every student in a caring way, whether he or she is sharing something personal or taking a content-related risk. Greet students with a smile every day: "Good to see you, Eric; how are you doing?" When you call on students, affirm, affirm, and affirm again. Make eye contact, smile, and gesture with an open palm. Use response phrases that start with things like, "I love how you . . .," "I feel good hearing that you . . .," or "Wow, you just knocked that one out of the ballpark!"

If students give the wrong answer, remember to maintain emotional security and help enrich them (through positivity and skill building, rather than criticism) so they can give a better answer. You might say, "I love your energy. Thanks for jumping in. Let's grab some contributions from others too," "You're on a different track. Let me rephrase the question. I'm not sure if I'm getting to the heart of the question I want to ask," or "I think you know the answer. Let's sort this out. Tell me first what you remember about this."

When students offer answers (correct or not), acute insights, or even marginally plausible answers to difficult issues, how do others react? Instead of saying, "Hmm, OK," be sure to make eye contact and say, "Thanks for jumping in. I appreciate that." Always acknowledge and respect each and every comment, every time.

Make the Classroom Physically Safe

Students conserve their cognitive space when they feel physically unsafe in class. This means you can allow no bullying or harassment. Ensure that students sit with others in a group or on a team in which everyone feels protective of each member: "This is our team. We look out for each other." Reinforce caring, camaraderie, and teamwork.

Team roles, leadership, and a culture of camaraderie can be amazing for stress reducers (Wegner, Schüler, & Budde, 2014). You read that right: when teams work with each other, stress goes down (Berger, Heinrichs, von Dawans, Way, & Chen, 2016). Talk openly about what bullying is, your level of tolerance for it (zero), and how members of the class will treat each other. Your class rule should be "Be nice," meaning that no one should make jokes, tease, or snicker when another student contributes. That, of course, includes you.

Chunk Material

Why is chunking more important to students from poverty than nonpoor students? Chronic stress impairs working memory. Working memory is the skill of holding pictures or sounds in your head and manipulating them to come up with answers or opinions. For your students, big chunks of information can be intimidating without content background or a strong working memory. When teachers cover content quickly, students are often overwhelmed. They may not have the background or the working memory to process it at the same pace, so they tune out. Break things into three- to six-minute chunks to produce sizable gains (Russell, Hendricson, & Herbert, 1984), and invest more time in retrieving previous content, not adding more. Chunking your content into smaller, bite-sized pieces helps students digest more easily; avoid bigger chunks that they simply forget.

Hit the Pause Button

On a micro scale, adding more pauses to the content is helpful (Ruhl, Hughes, & Schloss, 1987). Preview the content you'll cover that day for the class, and then pause. After the opening of your class, summarize it in one to two sentences, and then pause. Pause after any strong statement. At the beginning of the year (or semester), be blunt; simply tell students, "Write this down; it's important." Invite students to lean in and listen closely. Pause before and after an important thought. Soon your students will realize that the pause is a cue: this is important; write this down!

Unless you are building working memory daily, you'll need to adjust your teaching for students who are unable to manage their own cognitive load. Provide more time to make notes and point out when to do it. Say things like, "Grab your pens, and jot this down. You'll need to know it for later."

Stretch the Content

Research suggests that when teachers space learning out over time, students experience better quality of understanding and retrieval. For example, let's say you have a block of content that would take ten hours of instruction to do it justice. You could introduce this within two days at the elementary level or within two weeks at the secondary level. But it would be more effective to stretch it out more than that. Plus, research demonstrates how deeply the storage and retrieval of content or skills is affected by study time (Cepeda et al., 2009). Study time is more effective when stretched out over several days or weeks, not crammed into one day.

Spaced learning, also known as distributed practice, is the process of using repeated learning experiences, separated by spaces or timed gaps, for processing and application. The concept is simple: "Too much, too fast, it won't last." This factor ranks high with a 0.71 effect size (Hattie, 2009). Learning is massed when there's little or no gap in the stream of content. A continuous forty-five-minute lecture at the secondary level is an example of massed learning. You can do far more to enrich students' learning when you introduce the same content in five segments of nine minutes each over a week's time. In a classroom, this means you can sprinkle a unit or module of content in small segments, with student retrieval reviews, or formative assessments, built into your learning schedule.

Prime students for future learning by introducing tough concepts days and weeks in advance with previews and advance organizers. Then, after the unit is finished, refer back to the prior learning, using reviews a week later, and integrate it into the next unit. Spaced learning stretches out the learning over time. If you thought a unit would take two weeks, allow it to take three to four weeks, and overlap it with the prior and upcoming units. However, of course, not all teachers have this sort of freedom or latitude with their planning. Teach 85 percent of the content during the middle two weeks. Teach 15 percent during the extended first and last week (use the remaining time to teach the previous or next unit). In my experience, this is harder but well worth it.

Spaced Relevance

Here we combine two terms: *spacing learning* and *relevance*. Spaced relevance is most effective when teachers use it every other day or at the middle of the period between content introduction and testing to enhance retrieval (Cepeda et al., 2009). Distributed learning (spread out) trumps massed (bunched up into a short period) learning. Students' recall improves especially when you add content relevance (Sartori, Lombardi, & Mattiuzzi, 2005). See figure 9.3. In figure 9.3, we begin with a body of

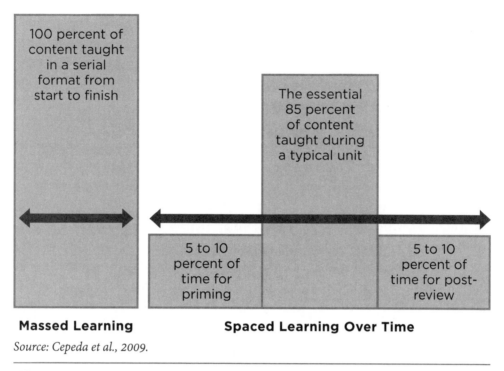

Source: *Cepeda et al., 2009.*

Figure 9.3: Spaced learning over time.

content. In one case (on the left), the content is taught at once. To the right, the content is broken into three chunks (preview, main body, and a post-review synthesis). The best review is retrieval, not just looking at familiar content. Give students time to think and figure out what they know instead of looking it up. In short, just studying is poor learning, and adding retrieval makes for strong learning.

Tools to Strengthen Retrieval

When we teach well, we bring students into the content, and they understand it well. But there's another critical piece to the academic puzzle: recalling learning at test time. For many, learning and recall are the same. Many believe that if we learn it, we should be able to recall it. But a large amount of what we learn is implicit (not taught to us explicitly) so we only retrieve it with a cue. "What's the name of the cross street near where you live?" That simple cue gives you the important difference: memory is what the brain stores; recall is what you can retrieve when you need it.

The gap between those two is mediated by frequency of use, relevance, and intensity of the memory. You can recall a lot when the stress is low and there's friendly banter full of prompts and cues for prior memories. A family reunion or brainstorming in a classroom is a social vehicle that prompts our recall. But retrieval is different. Retrieval is the ability to generate the information without prompts such as social clues, multiple-choice tests, or verbal prompts. Retrieval practice at school strengthens memories the most.

Retrieval practice is a huge, yet enormously underused, tool to strengthen recall. It simply means giving students time to retrieve prior learning by just writing it down without studying or looking at notes. Most teachers ask questions or give quizzes, but some students simply want to look up the answers. That's bad for the brain; no hard work often means no learning.

In a study involving sixth-grade social studies and eighth-grade science students, there were two groups of students. The control group learned the content and followed it by reviewing and studying the answers on slides, then the group was tested (Roediger, Agarwal, McDaniel, & McDermott, 2011). Students in the experimental group received the same content (for the same length of time, at the same time). Afterward, they were asked to retrieve the information on paper through study. The results showed that those who only studied by rereading the text averaged 79 percent correct, and those who did brief retrieval practice (from eliciting the content from memory) scored on average 92 percent. This shows a clear choice: introduce content and give students retrieval practice to recall information from their studying. For this study, it was a difference between a C+ and an A–. See figure 9.4.

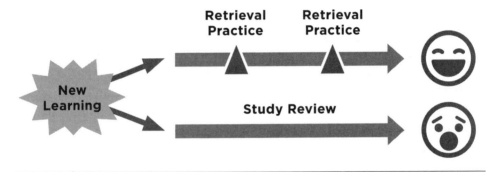

Figure 9.4: Enhancing learning—retrieval versus study review.

Why do retrieval work and studying sometimes fall short? It's simple; most learners confuse familiarity and fluency with their ability to retrieve the content. Those are separate functions. Looking at familiar content is easy; it may seem as if you could recall it. But retrieval, which means eliciting the stored content without prompts, is hard mental work that strengthens the memory more than looking something up. Spelling tests are a good example of familiarity versus retrieval. Students can think they know the words after rereading them several times, but when tested, they may not. It is the hard work of retrieval that helps cement the accurate memory. If a student looks up the right answer beforehand, he or she defeats the purpose of the activity.

In your classroom, retrieval practice can take the shape of:

- Using self-quizzing time
- Asking students to do the hard work of selectively remembering what they learned earlier (or the day before)

- Spacing out the retrieval practice

- Letting students practice the learning several times

- Using different problem types (such as for word and number problems, lists, narratives and characters, facts, inferences, and cause and effect)

- Varying the process by making the retrieval social one day (with a partner or group) and independent the next (writing from memory)

- Using flipcharts for retrieval one day, and the next day using verbal instruction

Switching up the use of verbal and nonverbal strategies is effective. Using more nonverbal strategies helps to represent the learning differently (using the body, showing the learning, gesturing, or building it). Students can choose from among many ways to represent learning. Give them choices, and let them choose (such as from creating a cartoon, tree diagram, swim-lane chart, mind map, Venn diagram, bubble map, storyboard, cause-and-effect chart, flow chart, tables, or graphs).

Simply creating a visual map (graphic organizer) can boost retention high enough to contribute to student achievement from one to even two years of gains (Petty, 2009).

Here are two nonverbal ways to enrich students' recall of your content.

Use Visual Organizers

Use visual organizers such as mind maps, time sequences, concept pattern organizers, target diagrams, cartoons, Venn diagrams, tree diagrams, flowcharts, cluster maps, spider webs, continuum diagrams, concept maps, or descriptive pattern organizers. David Hyerle's (1996) book *Visual Tools for Constructing Knowledge* is excellent. Use these first as a pretest. Ask students to show what they know in ten minutes. Then, use the visual organizer to preassess prior knowledge. You can also use them for a formative assessment or summative assessment. Using these can produce effect sizes on student achievement of up to 1.2 (Marzano, 1998). Visit **go.SolutionTree.com/instruction** for a sample visual organizer you can use with students.

Gesture the Content

When teachers gesture key concepts, it allows students to hear what they're saying without having to visualize it. This may mean acting out or showing something just through the use of expressions or hands alone. The idea is to avoid speaking or showing a picture. Gesturing also has a solid basis in helping learning last (Cook, Mitchell, & Goldin-Meadow, 2008). Here are two examples: (1) to illustrate a big idea, ask students to stretch their hands way out to either side, (2) if one thing is way better than another, stand on a chair, point to the ceiling, and balance by touching a chair or student's shoulder. Gesturing reduces students' cognitive load and helps them learn (Ping &

Goldin-Meadow, 2010). Another activity is to ask students to identify the two to three main concepts of the lesson. They can brainstorm a list of potential ideas first, and then vote on them within their teams. Next, take the top two and create a physical way to demonstrate them.

The gestures students spontaneously use when explaining a task typically predict whether they will subsequently learn that task. Gesturing reflects a student's readiness to learn and plays a role in learning the task as well as the relationships of the content areas. Students using gestures to learn mathematics had 90 percent retention (versus 30 percent with no gestures), affirming that it helps memory (Cook et al., 2008). For example, you can use movement in mathematics to gesture the numbers, signs, equations, and answers (go to www.mathandmovement.com for ideas). Mathematics is a subject that students can actually love when taught well.

Quick Consolidation

Enriching means we'll have to be cognizant of the whole student if he or she is going to succeed. Cognitive load issues are huge with students from poverty. You may see and hear students in class who often seem distracted, unfocused, inattentive, and impulsive. Please try to drop these labels and judgments. They are common symptoms of a stress disorder. When the brain is consumed with survival, it uses up mental space it needs for academic excellence. You can either notice the issue and make the students the problem or change what you do and help them succeed. I promise your results will be better if you make building relationships and ensuring safety (cognitive, emotional, and intellectual) your number-one priorities. Then, build in the strategies that will help with memory and recall. These are ways you can enrich students to help them succeed.

CHAPTER 10

DEVELOP BETTER THINKING SKILLS

Doing everything in your power to enrich students' brains means reviewing the effects of poverty and continuously making connections. Poverty commonly affects the cognitive skill base in students that schools value, which includes attentional skills, speed of processing, and memory. But what are thinking skills, and can we teach them?

Thinking skills are a broad category. When we say that a student has good thinking skills, we often include the ability to pay attention; exert a strong locus of control; evaluate, process, prioritize, and sequence content; hold information in short-term memory; compare and contrast; extrapolate and use working memory while manipulating the content; and finally, defer gratification until the answers are necessary. That's more than half a dozen subskills and one reason why thinking skills are a challenge to teach.

Because it is nearly impossible to declare a universal thinking formula, the process of teaching students to think critically is far more effective if you empower students to do the right type of thinking at the right time. Cognitive expert Daniel Willingham (2008) defines *critical thinking* as having effectiveness, novelty, and self-direction. Critical thinking is only effective when students avoid common mistake biases (seeing only one side of an issue, discounting new evidence that runs counter to their ideas, failing to use basic rules of logic, or failing to look for evidence). Willingham (2008) asserts the thinking must be novel, not a memorized formula from a familiar situation. He also says critical thinking is self-directed; the thinker must be doing the thinking, not following a teacher's or coach's prompts. This understanding is what real enrichment is all about.

Many believe thinking skills are genetic. Parents love to say their children are smart. After all, there is a genetic component to nearly every human trait. Among the broad category of thinking skills, one subset is reasoning skills. But reasoning skills, like many other thinking skills, have a low effect size of 0.23 (Plomin, Haworth, & Davis, 2009). The effect size is statistically significant, but not even moderate as far as effect sizes go. Robert Plomin, one of the world's foremost geneticists, says, "Despite our three-stage study demonstrating enrichment of associations for general cognitive ability, the genetic variants that make up the heritable component of intelligence remain elusive" (as cited in Davis et al., 2010, p. 762). Plomin is saying the genetic subsets are hard to find in our genes. Yes, there is heritability for intelligence, but it is negligible in those from poverty (Tucker-Drob, Rhemtulla, Harden, Turkheimer, & Fask, 2011).

In fact, a good bit of evidence shows thinking skills can be taught, if you know how to do it right—and if you believe in the enrichment mindset, which says you can change and grow.

Evidence on Teaching Thinking Skills

Thinking skills are part of a student's clear path to graduation. Reasoning is an important thinking skill that can and should be taught with two specific rules in place: (1) having a high-performing teacher and (2) transferring the skill to dissimilar material weakens results (Barnett & Ceci, 2002; Reeves & Weisberg, 1994). Tools for optimal reasoning include the following.

- Seek (read, listen, and experience).
- Apply standards (discriminate input).
- Interpret and define the true problem.
- Analyze (by both whole and part).
- Compare and contrast positions.
- Check claims, evidence, and biases.
- Use inductive and deductive reasoning.
- Make predictions and inferences.
- Translate, explain, and take action.

The preceding list offers generic steps to teach and learn reasoning skills. In the next section, I'll spell out some specific strategies. This is not a formula but rather a set of reminders. Remember, teach thinking strategies with the context of the content you have. In other words, these skills have moderate to low transfer. Use your own subject matter and foster the skills that apply to your class. A student may mount an argument against a nominal issue, missing the bigger point. Teach students to use every tool on this list so they'll be able to learn the right tools for the right problems. This means teaching thinking skills across the curriculum.

Building reasoning skills takes willingness to try the process out and positive belief in your students. These findings support adopting a deliberate (planned with enough time and quality feedback) practice approach when learning informal reasoning (Barnett & Ceci, 2002; Reeves & Weisberg, 1994). There are many simple strategies you can employ in the classroom. The following are some of my favorite problem-solving paths.

Teach the Language of Thinking

Start with the basics of thinking—language—as some students need this background knowledge. This is the foundation for reasoning. The words we choose represent the concepts and details of any reasoning we do. Without the correct word (or gesture, object, or other representation) to represent our thoughts, we cannot be accurate or complete in our thinking. Explain the following phrases, and then check for understanding.

- "Here's what this argument means."
- "What other words are similar to *means*?"
- "If I cut up a dessert into smaller pieces, what am I doing?" (Depending on the words your students use, question them: "Does *cut* mean *divide*, does *share* mean *divide*, does *split up* mean *divide*?")

Seek Out Information to Solve a Problem

First, encourage students to become curious learners and seek out relevant information. You can be a great role model for this process. In class every week, share something that fascinated you. If their role model is excited about learning, it will become contagious. Second, help them discriminate between various types of information. Show them that the source of the material is key to understanding the type of reasoning to apply. The source may be a friend or a scholarly journal. Next, show students how to choose the correct problem to solve or argue. Here is a basic seven-step framework for defining the true problem and honing students' reasoning skills.

1. Define the true problem.
2. List personal biases and how to overcome them.
3. Generate two to five potential paths to take.
4. Evaluate and select pathways, and then pick one to start.
5. Implement solutions.
6. Analyze results and try another, if needed.
7. Summarize what you have learned.

Visit **go.SolutionTree.com/instruction** for an infographic on biases that can affect students' decision making. Help them identify their own past biases to get to a clear thinking pathway. Teach the many ways to approach a problem. Make a list of the types of problems to solve, and share how you would use different approaches with each. Model how to approach a problem, and let them solve a similar one.

Ask the Right Questions

Teach students to ask the right question so that they invest their time effectively. Give students a word problem to solve. Then, ask each student to pair up and discuss the question, "Which is the real problem to solve?" Ask your questions from multiple perspectives before deciding on the problem. "What would she say is the problem? What about him?" Next, ask students to provide evidence for their claims (back it up). Call on students to find out the best way to solve the problem. Sometimes they are off track and solving a related (but irrelevant) problem.

Form Effective Arguments

Teach students that reasoning usually requires putting on different "hats" to see things from different points of view. Edward de Bono (1999) suggests six *thinking hats* (overview, information, benefits, creativity, feelings, and caution) to diversify thinking. You might also suggest using someone else's perspective ("I am going to look at this problem as a scientist, an ecologist, a businessperson, a mathematician, a politician, a church leader, or a school student" or "I'm going to approach this problem from the perspective of urgency, public good, private good, long-term importance, short-term importance, cost versus value, probability of complete success, or public relations)." As you can see, there are endless ways to approach a problem. Your role is to help students get used to understanding any problem from more than one position.

As a thinking tool, walk through each of the following five steps, and when students seem comfortable with the process, have them pair up and take opposing views.

1. Predict the main lines of argument (for or against), and for or against any salient alternative.

2. Summarize the supporting evidence that backs up each argument.

3. Analyze the opposing views and merits of other arguments.

4. Explain the reasoning for why one idea or bit of evidence is better than another.

5. Formulate tentative conclusions to be inferred and what would change minds.

For example, ask a student to take the viewpoint of someone who just arrived in America and another student to speak as a multigenerational resident, or one to be progressive and another to be conservative. Perhaps students could take the perspective of a dove and hawk in the military.

Deconstruct Constructs

Teach students how to use, critique, and deconstruct constructs. *Constructs* are shared abstractions (ideas or theories) among people. These might include phrases such as *the typical family* or *today's students*. Understanding reasoning skills means we must understand the essence of a topic. The essence in part comprises a concept's unique qualities or properties. In other words, what makes that word (or idea, thing, or person) unique? Students must work hard mentally to do this, and they'll need guidance from you. What properties can we agree on for your students from poverty?

For a classroom example, let's say the concept is *justice*. Let students partner up and make a list of their associations with that concept. Students (depending on grade level) might come up with words like *fairness*, *legal*, *police*, *retribution*, *courts*, *justice*, *civil rights*, and *laws*. They might divide issues of justice into clusters such as *society*, *house*, and *neighborhood*.

Soon, students will begin to see certain words define something very well. Justice takes on a whole new meaning for students when they see all the ways to understand it (or to lack understanding of it). For example, courtroom justice is different than street justice. Students can't reason without knowing how to relate to, connect, and deconstruct each construct.

Then, ask for the types of claims they are making about a word. Students may have personal experiences and narratives that enrich some of the concepts. This is the starting point for a fabulous writing assignment that gives students a stronger voice. Personal experience is a type of claim, and so is a peer-reviewed journal. Let them start with their own voice, and then ask them to organize their thoughts, bring in claims, and write the conclusion.

Use Argument Mapping

Next, it's time to illustrate and use visual thinking tools. Give students argument maps (such as a box-and-arrow or node-and-link diagram), which show the relationships, hierarchies, and links among all data pieces. (Rationale, www.rationaleonline.com, offers argument maps to support reasoning skills.) Argument mapping is semiformal, blending formal graph structure with natural language. You can think of it as addressing a design challenge: come up with a way to make a case and back it up with evidence. Researchers show that critical-thinking skills can be dramatically accelerated, with up to a 0.60 effect size, over one semester (van Gelder, 2015; van Gelder, Bissett, & Cumming, 2004). This suggests that argument mapping may foster college-prep thinking for K–12 students.

You might ask students to take their ideas and make a bubble map. They can put their key concept in the center. Ask them to make groups with new ways to divide up their words. When students add more concepts, it helps them see the breadth and depth of issues. Bubble maps help them start to identify the issues better based on relevance.

It's important to provide a model. You have a universe of learning in your head. You can't share it all at once, so what students need is not what you know (they can find that in a text or on the Internet) but *how* you know what you know. This requires that you think like a beginner and literally write out the steps that one could follow to think like you. Teachers often post a model for the writing process or for solving word problems on the wall. Using models is a fantastic idea if you explain, refer to, and use them often. The basic problem-solving thinking model for arguments is worth posting. See figure 10.1.

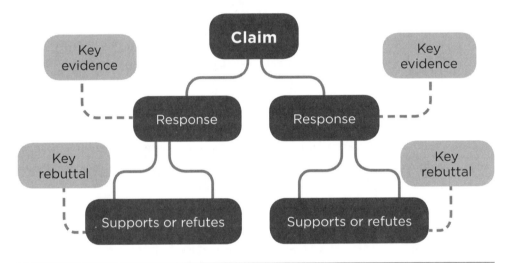

Figure 10.1: Basic problem-solving thinking model.

Remember, a model is an outline of a procedure. Over time, a more advanced learner may embellish it or find shortcuts. But in the beginning, models can be priceless windows into the mental world of thinking skills. Using models is in my top-five list for smart cognitive skill building.

Use Student Verbalization

Ask students to talk through the process of solving a problem. This allows them to better reflect on and receive feedback for their thinking process to improve its quality. This process ranks high in contributing to student achievement. It has a 0.64 effect size, putting it in the top 25 percent of all factors (Hattie, 2009). Here's how to use this strategy.

1. Students select the problem at their seats and work with partners to talk through it both before they try it out and during the actual problem solving.

2. Students stand as they share their thinking during a whole-class discussion; you help guide them to think more deeply or find more useful ways of understanding a topic.

Use a Reasoning Questioning Schema

A reasoning questioning schema ensures you always start at the beginning and drill deeper into the thinking-skill area. For example, you might begin with what students already know. Consider the following four question formats (Marzano & Simms, 2014).

1. **Discovery questions:** "Let's review what we have explored so far" or "Let's do word association: when I say *ecosystem* you say _____."

2. **Essential questions:** "How do ecosystems impact your life and why do they matter?" Use McTighe and Wiggins's (2013) book *Essential Questions*.

3. **Elaborative questions:** "What makes ecosystems different than an experiment in a lab?"

4. **Evidence-gathering questions:** "What photographic evidence or science journals support your case?"

You and I would never argue that the preceding schema is the only or best set of steps. But it can work for students, if you allow it to work.

Use Powerful Questions

Teachers whose students struggle with reasoning typically ask one or two questions, often those that probe for answers like, "What is . . . ?" or "Which of the . . . ?" Teachers who excel at teaching reasoning use a sequence of questions to develop thinking. You might hear the following questions. Visit **go.SolutionTree.com/instruction** for a reproducible of these questions.

- "Tell me again please, what claim are you making?"
- "What's your evidence for saying that?"
- "Can you connect what (another student) just said to your comments? Do you feel different or the same; do you agree or disagree?"
- "If that happened, what might happen next?"
- "What are probable causes for that?"
- "Why did they do it this way, and can you think of other ways to do it?"

You will want to have your own process for using powerful questions. The ones I use include the following.

- Provide sufficient wait time (five to ten minutes).
- Model how to answer (say, "That is true because of . . .").

- Never accept easy answers (such as, "Yes," or "No," or "I don't know"). Challenge students to do more. Ask them to listen to the next two students and then make a fresh guess.

- Keep higher-order question stems posted and refer to them often. Ensure everyone participates, and thank each student for contributing. ("How would you respond to the criticism that _____?" "In what way could you explain that to a newcomer?" "What could be an alternative explanation for your conclusion?" "What might an outsider to this issue say?" "What is your strongest argument that this is true?" "If it was false, what would be the most likely reason?")

You can say, "Thanks for jumping in" or "I love your ideas." The core understanding here is simple. Reasoning skills, one of the absolute basics of higher-order thinking and executive functioning, are a teachable process. If you fail to teach them, your students may miss out for the rest of their lives on the skills you take for granted. Now, let's take your students to an even higher cognitive level.

Support Top-Flight Thinking Skills

Over time, you'll become better at asking thinking questions that develop student brains. But to get to the highest levels, students also need to learn how to ask better questions. In *Making Thinking Visible: How to Promote Engagement, Understanding, and Independence for All Learners*, authors Ron Ritchhart, Mark Church, and Karin Morrison (2011) discuss the necessary scaffolding to enrich cognitive capacity. This work is the result of Harvard's Project Zero.

Making Thinking Visible gives teachers a simple format for teaching thinking. The authors suggest and encourage using specific thinking routines every day to develop the skills. The three categories of routines are: (1) introducing and exploring ideas, (2) synthesizing and organizing, and (3) digging deeper. Give your students practice in writing and asking their peers questions. There's nothing new here, but it is the respect you show for your students, and hence, the culture of thinking, that gets fostered. Remind students that the questions they develop will bring the answers they want.

Teach your students thinking and questioning tools such as:

- Identifying what they know and what they need to ask more about

- Creating a circle of varied viewpoints and questions

- Employing statements like, "I used to think _____, and now I think _____."

- Fostering two opposing views and a verbal tug-of-war with questions
- Using sentence-phrase-word representation of meaning and new questions (students explain their thinking in one sentence, then shorten to a phrase, and then a word)

To develop top-flight thinking skills, start with a simple format, such as a three-step model: (1) claim, (2) support, and (3) question (then, "What else is true or not?"). Once students know the model, you'll be able to expand to use or add other models.

As you have seen, reasoning is actually a core cluster of skills, not just for school survival, but of course, for life. Students are not reasoning when they copy, recall, or complete simple tasks. Reasoning requires that students take information through a sequence of steps that allows them to understand it differently, find relevance, and change the representation of the information into a meaningful goal. You now have the tools to help them.

Quick Consolidation

This chapter asks whether thinking skills are genetic (fixed mindset) or if they can change (growth mindset). The evidence shows that reasoning can be, and should be, taught. I also showed you evidence that you can successfully teach reasoning if it is content specific. You saw a list of cognitive tools to use for any type of reasoning activity, although not all are mandatory for every situation.

Different strategies fit different problems and situations. For example, while teaching a unit, you might learn to ask different questions. After each brief lecture component, give students time to develop and ask questions. Any time a teacher complains that his or her students are not good at thinking, remember that the greatest probability is that no one has ever taught them to think. When you build thinking into each part of a classroom, and when you show an interest in and respect for students' thinking, then they begin to build cognitive capacity. This means you'll become committed to the expression of each student's ideas, questions, and observations.

As you engage the enrichment mindset, you assume that students can learn tough, complex thinking tasks. You can be the one teacher who helps students succeed because you cared enough, had confidence in them, and took the time to build their cognitive capacity. Be the one who stands out in students' minds as someone who cared and taught them the hard stuff they can use for the rest of their lives.

CHAPTER 11

ENHANCE STUDY SKILLS AND VOCABULARY

Our commitment is to develop the enrichment mindset. To do that, we must remember that the effects from poverty start early on. From kindergarten on, the achievement gap widens between poor students and their middle-class peers, unless they catch up quickly—by the K–2 years (Palardy & Rumberger, 2008). Most students from poverty end the K–5 experience right where they started it: behind grade level. Let me restate this: teaching students learn-to-learn skills (the steps and skills to start as a novice and become an expert), and particularly anything that builds cognitive capacity, is critical. Without your support, students may not graduate. Your thinking here is simple; you must tell yourself, "If I don't better prepare my students, they may not make it."

This chapter focuses on two brain builders (study skills and vocabulary) that are core for enriching students. Before we get started, consider this: the symptoms that you see in your classroom when students lack these skills are usually apathy, discouragement, and low motivation. Those symptoms might lead an unknowing teacher to believe the student has an attitude or effort problem. After all, those are common. But often, especially with the poor, you're just as likely to see a lack-of-skill problem or a relevance issue. Before you ever judge a student, hold up a mirror, and ask yourself if you have tried all the options first.

Contextual Study Skills

I begin this section with a word of caution about study skills. The use of specific study aids (such as study guides, study procedures, and advanced organizers like text outlines) shows very promising results with large effect sizes (0.77 and up; Petty, 2009). But there are also studies that show little or no effect (Petty, 2009). So, why the big range in effectiveness? It depends on how specific the subject is. When the study process is fairly general and more abstract, the research consensus is that direct teaching of general, all-purpose study skills is not highly effective—about a 0.45 effect size (Petty, 2009). See figure 11.1.

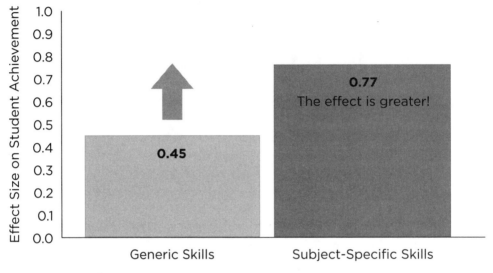

Source: Hattie et al., 1996.

Figure 11.1: Subject-specific study skills.

Generic study skills can build confidence and improve attitude, but the effect size is unremarkable (Hattie, 2009). Research on study skills is complicated because (Biggs, 1987) of the following.

- There is no research agreement on which strategies or tactics comprise core steps, processes, or a common body of study skills tactics. This makes comparison very difficult.

- Metacognitive interventions that focus on self-monitoring can increase the effectiveness of study tools.

- Cognitive skills usage also has an affective side, which fuels students' self-concept and the motivation and persistence with which they will use a strategy.

Here we focus on what we do know that works really well. First, while there are individual tactics that do have strong effect sizes, it's refreshing to have a unified system that raises the likelihood of success. Figure 11.2 illustrates the top study process achievement boosters (Petty, 2009). These boosters should be in every student process

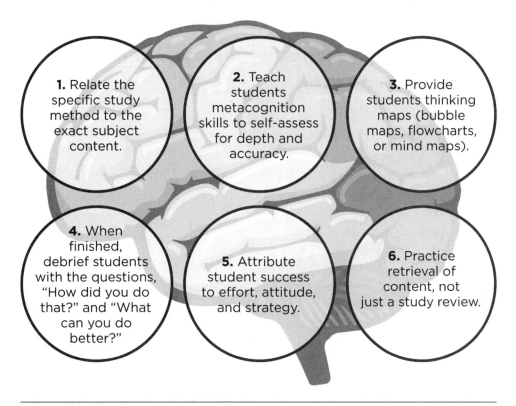

Figure 11.2: High-impact study skills.

for subject-specific study skills that you will develop, with help from your colleagues. Each high-impact study skill is powerful by itself. But when combined with the others, you will have the means to develop amazing learners. Walk students through each study step as a class. Then, let them do the step in pairs. Finally, when they have gained confidence, allow them to solve problems on their own. But why make the study skills so subject specific?

The use of study aids like summarizing and note taking can bump up progress with a 1.0 effect size (Marzano, 2001) or two years' worth of gains. Structural aids are strategies that show the specific framework of what students are learning. These aids, which might be an outline or other visual aid, have a strong effect size of 0.58 (but can go up to over 1.1), as 0.50 is one year's gain in academic achievement.

Following are some other helpful study aids.

Relational Study Aids

Relational study aids (bubble maps, mind maps, Venn diagrams, and so on) help students see connections between the content and how to learn it. They are also underused and highly valuable. In this case, figures 11.3 and 11.4 (page 98) are two forms of a study

Mathematics Problem Solving

1. **Begin with the right attitude.**
   "I can do this!"

2. **Determine problem type.**
   Picture it, or turn it into a story.

3. **Select a strategy.**
   Articulate it or draw it out, and then predict the likely outcome.

4. **Try out your strategy.**
   Make a rough draft of your potential solution.

5. **Check your work.**
   Use a calculator, reverse solve it, ensure it answers the question, check your prediction, and ask if it makes sense.

6. **Decide.**
   If your answer is not correct, redo steps 2, 3, and 4.

7. **Celebrate and affirm success.**
   Notice and affirm your strategy, effort, or attitude.

Figure 11.3: List of mathematics study steps for secondary students.

Mathematics Problem Solver

Attitude! ⇨ Decide problem type. ⇨ Select strategy. ⇨ Test-run idea; then use it. ⇨ Check your work!

Figure 11.4: Flowchart of mathematics study steps for elementary students.

skill tool for a mathematics class. The elementary flowchart in figure 11.4 is more reader friendly, but both of these forms are helpful (versus using none at all).

Although other strategies can work well, the best strategy is to teach study skills in a subject-specific context. Use specific study aids that illuminate the structure of your content and its core relationships. The effect size for this strategy is much higher (0.77) than using a generic strategy; that's a year and a half of gains (Petty, 2009).

Work collaboratively with your school teams to create simple, five- to seven-step grade-level study guides for your key content areas and incorporate them into the instructional process of retrieving the material a day or week later. These should include reading for depth, lower-level mathematics (addition, subtraction, multiplication, and division), and science. Making posters of the guides and referring to them in class are also helpful.

Strategies for contextual study skills are powerful ways to build better brains. It is rare that students have teachers like you that set out to plan, develop, and follow through on practical efforts to help students become smarter. Now, all of the cognitive skills have to work in parallel with another process. Since students often struggle with building an academic vocabulary, we'll want to add that to our school day.

Vocabulary Skill Building

The vocabulary of students growing up poor is typically smaller than those of their middle- and upper-class peers, which places their academic success at risk. Children from poverty commonly receive less cognitive stimulation, which starts impeding academic progress (Ginsborg, 2006). Children from low–socioeconomic status home environments begin school with huge, multiyear vocabulary gaps, compared with middle- and upper-class children (Hart & Risley, 2003). Children from families on welfare hear about 616 words per hour, working-class families hear about 1,251 words per hour, and professional families hear about 2,153 words per hour. By age three, this leads to a word gap of about thirty million between low-income and upper-income students (Hart & Risley, 2003). When tested at age seven, high-performing students know and use an average of 7,100 root words, yet students in the lower quartile know and use 3,000 words. This gap (4,000-plus words) can only be closed when the student learns five more words a day (in addition to those typically learned at grade level) for four to five years (Biemiller, 2003).

See figure 11.5 (page 100). Your thinking should be simple; tell yourself, "If I don't enrich my students' vocabulary, they may not succeed."

Ensure strong academic and confidence gains with vocabulary building. When you help students learn ten to twelve new words (relevant to tested material) per week, the gains over a year average 33 percentile points or a huge 0.95 effect size (Marzano, 2001). It's also imperative that teachers help students catch up and teach words that aren't specific to tested material but are academically general: like *rigorous*, *reflective*, or *assess*. The evidence is clear that vocabulary building must form a key part of the enrichment experience for students. Start with a goal of three hundred vocabulary words per year or ten words weekly. Over twelve years, this builds a 3,600-word database of academically relevant vocabulary. Here's how to get started.

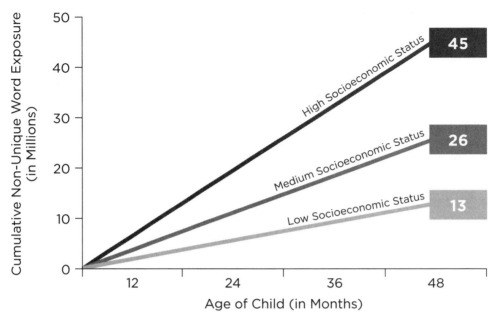

Source: Hart & Risley, 1995, 2003.

Figure 11.5: Early word exposure and socioeconomic status.

Role-Model

First, role-model the use of the word. Use the word in a sentence, and then ask students to predict the meaning. If they don't get it, keep using it in new sentences, and let them work with others until they figure it out by consulting a thesaurus and a dictionary. Once you think they have a general idea of the definition, ask students to write or talk through a restated meaning in their own words with a partner. Then, they make their own interesting and accurate sentence using the word. Finally, ask them to draw the word and share the drawing.

Use Big Words

Remember, use your big words! Research compared reading comprehension progress in middle school groups, using beginning-of-year and end-of-year scores across a variety of classrooms. The researchers recorded and analyzed the teacher's speech in those same classrooms. Students whose teachers used more sophisticated vocabulary in class significantly improved their reading comprehension as the year progressed (Gámez & Lesaux, 2015).

- Instead of saying "That's *bad*," say, "That's *invidious*."
- Instead of saying, "That's *great*," say, "That's *spectacular*."

- Instead of saying, "That's *hard*," say, "That's *formidable*."

Use Direct Vocabulary Instruction

Marzano suggests using direct vocabulary instruction with a research-based, six-step process (Marzano & Simms, 2013).

1. **Demonstration:** Provide a description, explanation, or example of the new term.

2. **Verbal:** Ask students to restate the description, explanation, or example in their own words.

3. **Nonverbal:** Ask students to construct a picture, symbol, or graphic representing the term or phrase. Post these on a word wall with rich adjectives for writing and content-related words the class is focusing on.

4. **Engagement:** Give students activities that help them add to their vocabulary knowledge.

5. **Reciprocal teaching:** Periodically ask students to discuss the terms with one another.

6. **Use of games:** Involve students in games that allow them to play with terms.

By the way, the use of gesturing and other nonverbal strategies (mind mapping, models, and so on) for learning and teaching vocabulary has a huge 2.27 effect size—over four years' worth of gains (Marzano, 1998). Ask students to pair up and demonstrate each new word, using words and gestures to help remember it.

Give students chances (through class discussion or assignments) to use all the words of the week. Teachers can use fun celebrations each time a student uses a word of the week. For example, every time it happens, the whole class stands up and says, "Oh, yes! I love this!" or add partner or team cheers to celebrate. In the following weeks, engage cooperative groups or student teams to review random vocabulary words from the comprehensive list.

Quick Consolidation

This chapter focused on learn-to-learn skills. Study skills and vocabulary are two huge difference makers in the potential success of students from poverty. Either your students will have a good chance at college or not. With study skills and vocabulary skills, your students can stand tall among the competition for a job. I am certain that you can understand the effect these strategies have on student achievement. To enrich learners, it's important for teachers to say, "I will grow my students in any way I can with core study skills and vocabulary."

Please, while this is fresh in your mind, lock in on something from this chapter, add it to your lesson plan, and make it part of your menu for next week. You've got students who just hope to have a great teacher this year. Are you that teacher?

CHAPTER 12

BUILD BETTER MEMORY

As we've seen, the human brain can change. Students from poverty can grow new brain cells, make connections, and hence, develop a superb memory. This supports the purpose of intentional brain building and not sorting students, making excuses, or feeling sorry for them. What cognitive skills would give you the greatest return on the investment of your time? Strong examples might include teaching writing, reading, reasoning, memory, and study skills. Those are all great, but which do you think is best? Please take this brief quiz.

> Question: What factor, when tested at age five, is a greater predictor of student success at age eleven than even a student's IQ?
>
> a. Vocabulary   d. Working memory
>
> b. Attitude   e. Reading skills
>
> c. Mathematics skills f. Motivation

The answer sounds like it must be pretty important, right? Yes, it is important. The correct answer is working memory (Alloway & Alloway, 2010). Additionally, there are predictive links between students' tested working memory skills when starting school and their subsequent mathematics achievement in later years (Passolunghi, Vercelloni, & Schadee, 2007). Why else is memory building so important? The biggest reason is that no matter how much vocabulary students learn, if they forget it they're still in trouble. No matter how many thinking skills they've learned, they still have to remember what to say. This is key for the enrichment mindset: all the strategies work together. When we enrich one part of a student's life, we say, "What else does the student need for success?"

In this chapter, we'll introduce strong memory builders your students can use immediately.

Build Long-Term Memory

For decades, policymakers and teachers have rebelled against student memorization of content. Yet, every year, we expect students to memorize rules (grammar), procedures, numbers, tables (science), themes, styles, authors (literature), and relevant facts (every subject). Curiously, we want teachers to strengthen reasoning skills, but we are not supposed to teach the memory skills that students need to base their reasoning skills on. You may have heard, "We teachers should focus on learning, not memory," but real-world experience (and the science) disagrees. So how do we reconcile this by focusing on long-term memory skills, not rote memorization? It is simple: teach the tools up front in your classes and from then on, students will use them with small amounts of encouragement, because they will see the benefit. It's not your focus during instruction, but fewer students will have a tough time remembering learning when they have specific memory-building tools.

The fact is, our memories comprise who we are, what we know, and where we are going. Most teachers assess a student who doesn't have a good memory as a poor learner. How many students knew their content, but did not recall it at test time? What does this have to do with students from poverty? Students growing up in poverty are more likely to have weaker long-term and working memory skills than middle-class students (Noble, Norman, et al., 2005).

Every grade level requires a foundation of learning from the previous year (that's long-term memory). School testing requires background knowledge, which is, in fact, long-term memory. When it comes to testing, if students have forgotten what they learned, it's tough to show that they ever learned it at all. Long-term memory is the foundation for much of what you know. Let's get real about this. Memory is important, and if you don't teach it, students will underperform.

In one study, students from low- and middle-income families received neurocognitive testing. The biggest difference between the kindergartners from the two social classes was in the language areas, but the number-two difference was memory (Noble, Norman, et al., 2005). See figure 12.1 for the effect sizes of these cognitive functions. The simple bar graph suggests the greatest differences are in language (no surprise). But two of the next three are memory differences. Now you understand the importance of teaching both language and memory skills.

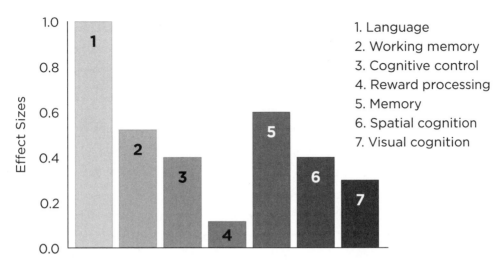

1. Language
2. Working memory
3. Cognitive control
4. Reward processing
5. Memory
6. Spatial cognition
7. Visual cognition

Source: Adapted from Noble, Norman et al., 2005.

Figure 12.1: Effect sizes of cognitive functions.

When I attended grades K–12, not one teacher taught me memory skills. No wonder school was so hard for me! Are there ways to strengthen student memory? Yes! Let's explore several of them. Check out the following strategies to build long-term memory skills.

- **Timing:** Pause every one to two minutes for ten to fifteen seconds while lecturing. Be sure to spread out the content over time and ensure students practice retrieving the content to strengthen memory.

- **Semantic:** Teach students how to turn a list of words into a useful acronym, abbreviation, or anagram (see page 106). In addition, discussing a topic and writing about it will strengthen memory.

- **Body:** Be sure to ask students to explain a concept while gesturing, and then draw the information using stick figures or diagrams and mind maps.

- **Feelings:** Use relevant emotions. The five most common emotions are joy, disgust, fear, anger, and sadness.

Consider the following strategies for enriching long-term memory.

Mnemonics

Near the top of the list of optimal long-term memory strategies is mnemonics (Hattie et al., 1996). Mnemonics is the broad use of memory strategies such as stories, loci (location-based memory), and peg words (a base list of numbers associated with a picture) with a huge effect size of 1.09.

Acronyms, Abbreviations, and Anagrams

An *acronym* is an abbreviation (word, letter string, or expression) formed from the first letters or parts of multiple words or phrases to form a new, easy-to-recall phrase. One common example is H-O-M-E-S as the letters representing the five Great Lakes (Huron, Ontario, Michigan, Erie, and Superior). But this strong effect only occurs when memory tools are specific to the subject being taught (Muncer & Knight, 2011).

In biology, teachers use the abbreviation K-P-C-O-F-G-S for kingdom, phylum, class, order, family, genus, and species. Remember this more easily with, "kids prefer cheese over fried green spinach."

Sometimes a new order of letters (anagram) will make it easier. For example, the eight parts of speech are noun, verb, adjective, adverb, pronoun, conjunction, preposition, and interjection, and the anagram is, "Cap van with a pi." Simply use the first letters of the terms you have to remember, and then rearrange the letters into an anagram. Sometimes, you'll need to change a word (to a similar one) if there's no anagram available with the letters you have. Visit Wordsmith (http://wordsmith.org/anagram) to create your own anagrams.

I recommend that you initially guide your students with a specific example, and when it's age appropriate, empower them to develop their own set of content-specific acronyms and anagrams. Among students with special needs, the effect size was a sky-high 1.47 for using mnemonics (Scruggs, Mastropieri, Berkeley, & Graetz, 2010). Acronyms can work well, but students rarely generalize the skill across various subject areas. This means if you help them learn to create content-specific strategies for each subject area, you'll see strong results.

Emotions

Make learning emotional, and the significance and permanence of the classroom experience will strengthen long-term memory (McGaugh, 2013). How do you do this? It's easy; ask yourself, "What usually engages emotions?" Use movement, competition, surprise, role plays, or suspense as part of the learning process to help embed the learning emotionally for long-term memory. Using highly relevant content can help students care about or connect with what you're teaching. Emotions at the middle range (not too strong or not too weak) can support a better memory. For example, a science teacher wants to show what happens when you combine a small amount of crushed saltpeter, charcoal, and sulfur at a 6-1-1 ratio (by weight). She mixes them in a mortar, moistened for safety, and grinds them together with the pestle for about ten minutes. Then, she ignites the mixture (it's gunpowder)—the emotions of surprise and fear will help students remember the activity. The emotional memory is for the gist of what happened, not for a list of details about it.

Music

Use music to hook students' interest in a topic. We have all had the experience of learning content in school with a song (such as learning the alphabet). Just adding one song or hearing a musical component during instruction can help students learn the content. Need classroom songs about chemistry, social class, politics, animals, teenage angst, war, nutrition, geography, mathematics, or economics? The Green Book of Songs (http://greenbookofsongs.com) offers access to thousands of ideas. Teachers can simply google a topic needing a song, such as "What song can help me learn the fifty states?" (I suggest "Fifty Nifty United States.")

Students from poverty need their teachers to support the enrichment mindset because the more you enrich them using long-term memory strategies, the more they'll achieve. Next up, we focus on immediate memory types, which are just as important.

Build Short-Term and Working Memory

Successfully completing most tasks requires the effective orchestration of multiple types of executive function skills. *Executive functions* are the run-your-brain skills that include processing, memory, attention, and self-control. Here we address two types of your "instant" memory: both short-term and working memory.

Short-term memory is a cognitive skill that describes the mental processing necessary for storing temporary input. It is almost like a Cut and Paste computer function. You can store a small chunk, and then use it seconds later.

Our brain holds both two types of content in our short-term memory: sounds (words, music, and so on) and pictures (text, illustrations, photos, and so on). Many still believe the often-repeated and outdated research that says our short-term memory is seven items, plus or minus two (Miller, 1956).

However, there are two things to keep in mind. First, Miller (1956) was referring to chunks of information (which might contain multiple bits). Second, he was referring to the untrained mind. Research suggests that with younger students, the numbers are closer to one to three items, and in the more mature (yet untrained) brain, the number of items typically stored is two to four (Cowan, 2010). However, we can store and manipulate many more items in our brains with better strategies and skill building.

First, let's explore short-term memory. Fortunately, short-term memory is a teachable skill (Crone, Wendelken, Donohue, van Leijenhorst, & Bunge, 2006). As an example, for those who train their brain constantly, the memory becomes quite extraordinary. Each year, the World Memory Championships crown an international winner after a grueling, three-day event. An eleven-year-old boy, Chen Zeqi (World Memory Council, 2015), memorized the sequence of every card in fifteen decks of playing cards in just one hour (780 card placements). He did not win the overall championship, but his time will come (with practice). If you think these are simply smart or gifted students, think again. Short-term memory is teachable.

Using short-term memory means students can hold the information as if it is held in their hand while being used in the brain. But *working memory* means they can hold the Scrabble letters in their hand but also mentally arrange them into a word. Working memory not only holds information but allows you to manipulate it. For example, adding numbers in your head (unless you've already memorized them) requires you to manipulate figures (using working memory).

Reading requires your working memory to hold and develop the meaning of the first half of the sentence while you finish the second half. Working memory correlates with better reading skills and mathematics skills because students need to hold content in their heads and process it while using new content for comprehension and accuracy (Sesma, Mahone, Levine, Eason, & Cutting, 2009).

Yes, at age five, working memory is far more predictive of student success at age eleven than IQ (Alloway & Alloway, 2010). Pause and take that last sentence in one more time. A student's IQ has less to do with academic success than working memory. Students from disadvantaged backgrounds typically have a weaker short-term memory due partly to chronic stress exposure (Evans & Fuller-Rowell, 2013). To give you an idea of how important working memory training is, let's check the research.

There is considerable controversy about how much value and transfer there is from working memory training. One study reviewed twenty-three high-quality interventions, where working memory was taught, and examined the results (Melby-Lervåg & Hulme, 2013). The immediate effect size on all student achievement ranged from 0.72 to 0.84 (from over one to two years' worth of academic gains). The greatest effects are on the subset of younger students (a massive 1.41 effect size on students under ten)—over two years of academic progress.

Another study of grade 4 students showed moderate gains (Söderqvist & Nutley, 2015). Students in one classroom (experimental group) completed a computer-based working memory training (they used Cogmed). Students in another classroom received education as usual (control group). Researchers used the performance on nationally standardized tests in mathematics and reading both at the start and two years later. By grade 6, the experimental working memory reading group had improved to a moderately strong 0.66 effect size. In mathematics, the effect size was 0.58, and the academic success correlated with the training success improvements (Söderqvist & Nutley, 2015). You can teach these skills as part of everyday classroom strategies, using rigorous direct instruction (Holmes et al., 2010).

There are many simple ways to build short-term memory. The benefits your students get are proportional to the quality and duration of the memory activities you generate. Please use these every time you teach memory.

1. Set clear objectives, and develop an evidence procedure.

2. Use existing content for the learning.

3. Get buy-in before starting the activity.

4. Make the learning collaborative, competitive, or interdependent (not solo).

5. Ensure immediate, actionable feedback.

6. Narrow the task to:

    a. Class content

    b. Auditory or visual activities

    c. Language arts or mathematics and science

7. Begin with a quick, easy learning curve with quick successes.

8. Slowly increase challenge and complexity over time only when students are getting 95 percent or more success on memory tasks for three consecutive days. Continuously check for understanding using computers or partners.

9. Practice ten to fifteen continuous minutes a day, three to five days a week, for eight to twelve weeks.

10. Keep the practice fun, reminding students that hard work is good, and keep the short- and long-term goals in mind.

Using these approaches will help when teaching students to improve their short-term and working memory. To differentiate between short-term and working memory, see figure 12.2.

Short-Term Memory

Can you hold and recall the content in your head (as-is) for seconds or minutes?

Working Memory

Can you hold, recall, and then manipulate the content in your head for seconds or minutes?

Figure 12.2: Short-term versus working memory.

Consider the following specific strategies to build students' short-term and working memory.

Name Games

You can begin your school year or semester with memory activities. Start by doing the well-known name game. Students start the activity by standing in circles of four or five each. One person starts a sentence with his or her name and one characteristic ("My name is Eric, and Eric is tall"). The person to the right continues the introductions, adding his or her name and repeating the previous name ("Eric is tall, and my name is Diane, and Diane is kind"). Each new person repeats all previous student introductions. When a student can't keep up, the game simply starts over, with the last student as the first to go. After two weeks, repeat the name game with new circles of eight to ten, and then increase the group size over time. The goal is for every student to know every other student's name.

Vocabulary Builders

When teaching new vocabulary, you know the rules: use the words in sentences. Introduce the word with a definition, and ask students to define it to a partner in their own words. You use it in a sentence, and then students write out an example. Students share the word and definition, get a chance to draw it out, and quiz a partner. Once they know the words, it's time for memory builders.

First, ensure the students know the words spelled forward. Then, every student gets a partner. They stand and face each other. You can make this an auditory or visual activity. Each partner has a list of five to ten vocabulary words. Ensure the list is age appropriate and relevant to the content. One student begins with the first word on his or her list. He or she says the word, spells it, uses it in a sentence, and spells it again. Then, the partner has to spell it forward, use it in a sentence, and then spell it backward, using working memory.

Ask younger students (grades 2 through 5) to spell two- and three-letter words forward, then backward from memory. With older students (grades 6 to 12), start with three- to four-letter words. As students improve, add more letters, maintaining perfect accuracy as you build. Partners can also perform this activity using flash cards. Remember, this process requires slow building over time. Avoid starting first graders off with words like *Azerbaijan*. Consider adding one letter every two to four weeks. Simply change the variety, complexity, context, and content to keep it fresh. Students must be getting 95–100 percent correct over and over for a week (with three days of practice) before you bump up the word length. Use peer feedback or have student teams grade written work to determine whether students are ready. As noted, using anagrams is great practice. Teachers can give students three letters, and they have to form one or two words from the letters using their memory (not writing it down). For a resource on scrambled words, go to Enchanted Learning (www.enchantedlearning.com/english /anagram/numberofletters).

Number Strings

For working memory practice in mathematics, start with simple two- or three-digit number strings (using whole, positive numbers). Say these numbers to your class. Students repeat them back to you first in reverse order and then in order of smallest to greatest value. Keep each number string a sequence of unrelated digits. For example, here is a string of numbers: 364, 792, and 185. Do not say, "three hundred and sixty-four." Say, "three, six, four." Why? The three-digit number is one unit, but giving the numbers separately gives three separate memory units to store.

Then, as students get better, use four number strings such as 8,364; 3,792; and 4,395. Once you have shown your students how this activity works, they can partner up and develop skills one on one. This process is great for building mathematics competencies, because you can continually build the task in complexity and challenge. Over time, your students will be able to recite number strings as long as five or six digits at the lower-elementary level and eight to ten digits at the secondary level.

For a short-term memory activity, get your students to listen carefully as you say some numbers. Start with single numbers in a serial order. Then, use two-digit numbers, and build up slowly. Digits should be given at the rate of one per two or three seconds, no faster. Students repeat the numbers back to you (or a partner) to trigger short-term, auditory memory. For example, say "three" then "two." Students repeat "three, two." Now, ask them to repeat the numbers to you in reverse order; that's working memory (manipulating the sequence of the numbers mentally).

For younger students (grades K–2), the best to way to learn this skill is with simple objects. With physical reminders made of plastic or wood (or simply use small pieces of paper with the number written on it), let students practice doing this activity at their desks. Allow them to group two numbers, remember the numbers, regroup them, and then add a number to get better. Doing this in the physical world is great rehearsal for the mental world.

The secret to making this work is to start small and make the additions random and repeated. Only go at a rate at which 90 percent of the class can repeat all the numbers. Once you get to that level, practice backward recall. Over time, slowly build up the number chains. Based on my experience, this takes five to ten minutes, three to five times a week, for eight to twelve weeks, to show strong gains.

Number Manipulation

Here's a great activity you can do with your students to help them add, subtract, rearrange, group, multiply, divide, reverse, sequence, or compute in ways that require holding the number and manipulating. At the K–5 level, you can use positive single-digit whole numbers. Say one number to a student ("five"). The student then can add, subtract, multiply, or divide using that number and another positive single-digit whole number ("five minus three is two"). Keep this developmentally appropriate. Then, you take the answer and do your own calculations. You might say, "Two times four is eight." Then, the student says, "Eight plus one is nine." Then, you say, "Nine divided by three is three." Then, your partner says, "Three times two is six." When this is done with students in partners, it is great fun.

Your job is to keep the activity challenging. One way to do that is to have a third student act as a mathematics coach. That student listens to the students doing the mathematics and checks their work for accuracy. That student can also say when it is time to change the functions or number sets. At the secondary level, after a few weeks, the students can use positive, double-digit whole numbers. The idea is simple: do hard mental work, keep making it harder and more complex, get feedback on it, and have fun. Doing times activities makes it even more fun since many students will feel the fun competition.

Cadence Songs

Let's double up on our enrichment. We know that brief walks are good for our brain (Miller & Krizan, 2016; Schaefer, Lovden, Wieckhorst, & Lindenberger, 2010). With that, we will combine a short-term memory builder. Cadence songs are marching songs with a call-response format. They build camaraderie, unity, and auditory short- and long-term memory. At school, the student leader begins with a line, and the students repeat each one. Teachers can use these for classroom self-discipline, chores, new words, or character building. In the following example, a K–2 grade teacher says each single line, and then students repeat it. Over time, the teacher can start using two lines at a time.

Teachers can use an eight-line cadence song as a walking energizer or to prepare for recess or lunch. Students begin this by standing in line, ready to go. The K–2 teacher says the first line of the cadence, and then after each line, the students repeat.

- "Let's line up; it's easy to do." (*Students have their heads up and repeat.*)
- "Hands at my side, all stuck like glue." (*Students snap hands to sides and repeat.*)
- "Feet together; it's cool to see." (*Students look down and repeat.*)
- "You watch you, and I watch me." (*Students look at teacher and repeat.*)
- "We can walk real fast; we've got a plan." (*Students walk fast and repeat.*)
- "We can walk so slow; oh yes we can." (*Students walk slow and repeat.*)
- "1, 2, 3, 4! We make sure we're in a row." (*Students count and repeat.*)
- "Ready to go when the teacher says so." (*Students repeat.*)

Cadence songs must start out simple and fun. Over time, you'll be asking more and more as the students develop a better short-term memory.

Simon Says

A classic short-term memory game is Simon Says. Typically, Simon Says is a listening, attentional activity. The keys of this game are to keep it fun, start simple, and build slowly. A female teacher can even use the name Simone instead of Simon. Students are only to do something that Simon or Simone says to do.

To build working memory, first ensure that students know the regular format for Simon Says. Then, you'll mix up the directions by giving two commands at once or asking students to only follow the first of two commands. These activities invite students to listen closely (attentional skills) and hold words and actions in their heads (working memory practice). For example, you could say, "This time, Simon says, 'Follow the first of the two commands.'" "Simon says, 'Clap your hands.'" "Simon says, 'Stomp your feet.'" Students should only clap their hands and not stomp their feet.

Content Add-On Review Builders

At both the primary and secondary levels, students can write short sentences of up to five or six words. Their partners (or the next student in a small group) repeat the previous sentence, and then add a new sentence to it. But the new one must be a logical sequence. Add-on activities build memory; it's incremental learning at its best.

For example, in a history class, the first student in a team of five says, "The U.S. fought in South Vietnam." The second one says, "The U.S. fought in South Vietnam. South Vietnam was its ally." The next student repeats the previous sentences and adds another. In this way, students can review history and build auditory short-term memory.

At the K–5 level, you can review any topic: "A verb is an action word." The next student says, "A verb is an action word, like *run*." The next student repeats this and may add, "Adverbs modify the verbs, like 'She runs fast.'" The idea is review, repeat, and build memory.

Call-Response Songs

Some songs repeat a brief chorus line (like "Day-O"). Repeating longer segments builds memory skills. For younger students (grades K–2), use songs that keep building onto the song's lyrics (such as "Old MacDonald Had a Farm"). These are excellent for younger students, since ideally, students have to keep track of all the previous verses. Another classic is "The Twelve Days of Christmas."

Clapping Repeats

This activity requires no planning. In fact, the beauty is its simplicity. The teacher starts with a very simple clap in front of the class: "Clap-clap," and students repeat it. The teacher repeats the clap: "Clap-clap" and, once again, students repeat it. Next, the teacher starts a new one: "Clap-clap (pause) clap-clap," and students repeat it. The sequence is critical: the teacher starts very easy, and then repeats the activity. Use the challenge to boost motivation: "Last week we got to level three; let's go for level four this week." The teacher builds up slowly, often doubling back to ensure the skills are solid. With just a few minutes a day, any teacher can boost listening skills and short-term memory. Over time, students can lead the class in this activity as a privilege.

Word Boxes or File Folders

This activity builds both short-term memory and attentional skills. The teacher gives the class an imaginary word box, meaning that all of the words have to come from the same box. For example, with first graders, if the word box is *fruits*, you can only choose fruits and no other words. Students can start this activity with a partner. The one who goes first says a word from the fruit basket. If *fruit* is the title of the word box, the first word could be *pear*. The other partner repeats the word *pear* and adds a new word from the same "basket" such as *apple*. Then, the original partner repeats, *pear* and *apple* and adds *orange*. This process goes on, back and forth, until someone can no longer recall all the fruits in the basket. Then, it is time to start over with a new box.

In a K–5 mathematics class, the word box might be a certain type of number (prime, double digit, divisible by 5 or add 9 to the last one, and so on). In an English class, the box might be pronouns, and in science the box might be elements from the periodic table. Teachers can do this for five to ten minutes a day in any content area as a pretest for prior knowledge or a review. As students get better, they can do this in cooperative groups of four to eight students. Use your imagination; you can develop word boxes for any required learning and students can have fun and build their brains.

Repeat-After-Me Activities

A repeat-after-me activity goes this way. You say to your students, "Today we are going to learn three ways that wind affects our weather. How many ways did I just say?"

Give one to two sentences as initial directions to start a new task. Then, say, "Now, turn to your neighbor and repeat the directions, in your own words, as best as you can. Ready, go!"

Visual and Verbal Memory Quizzes

You say to students (who are in their usual cooperative groups or teams), "Point to a neighbor in your group who was here yesterday. Now tell him or her what colors he or she wore yesterday. Ready, go!"

You say to your students, "Yesterday, we posted our new vocabulary word for the day. Go ahead, talk it over with your neighbor, define it, and then write it down. As soon as you have it written, hold up your answer on the paper. Let's see what you got!"

Online Memory Training Resources

The following sites have proven brain-training software modeled after quality research. Jungle Memory (www.junglememory.com) is great for K–5 students. Scientific

Learning (www.scilearn.com) and BrainHQ (https://secure.brainhq.com) are both quality resources and terrific for secondary students. When you use Scientific Learning's Reading Assistant (www.scilearn.com/products/reading-assistant), students not only get better at reading but also better at paying attention, phonological processing, and working memory (Russo, Hornickel, Nicol, Zecker, & Kraus, 2010). One solid company, C8 Sciences (www.c8schools.com), will come to your school and put these cognitive skill-building strategies into action for your students.

Quick Consolidation

The enrichment mindset is an impressive approach for building your students' cognitive capacity. Cognitive strategies are so powerful that, by working in grade-level or subject teams, each teacher can focus on different areas at the secondary level. At the K–5 level, focus on building two new cognitive skills at each grade level. By the fifth grade, the students will truly be enriched. This was a full chapter, but then again, you were learning a core cognitive component of academic achievement: memory. Long-term, short-term, and working memory are critically important. We cannot in good conscience expect, or even hope, that students will learn it unless we stress the urgency and make it easy to implement. Short-term memory is highly predictive of student achievement for complex activities including language comprehension, problem solving, and learning (Engle, 2001), and it's strongly related to general intelligence (Conway, Kane, & Engle, 2003). I urge you to give your students memory training. It's that important. Now, lock in on something from this chapter, and make it part of your lesson plan. Your students are waiting for an amazing teacher to show up who will help them feel smarter.

CHAPTER 13

LOCK IN THE ENRICHMENT MINDSET

This chapter ties up the strategies on enriching the brain. Far too many teachers talk about what's wrong with students and how their poor upbringing makes them "less than" for life, but DNA is not destiny. The key is to develop the enrichment mindset, which shows that all brains can grow, including theirs.

Most of us deal with success pretty easily. We can internalize it and feel great as we swell up with pride or socialize it and show off with a new swagger. We may even dismiss success as an exception. But failure is more important to deal with, since it will guide much of your life. When students fail, how do you respond? Are you disappointed and find yourself looking for blame? When students fail, do you immediately use that as a gift and opportunity to grow? Do you model how to deal with mistakes in your class, or do you avoid them at all costs? What is your narrative about failure?

Change the Narrative, Change Your Teaching

In each chapter, I have invited you to listen to your own narrative about a part of your teaching. Here, you can choose to live the narrative of enrichment and growth, not judgment. The preceding chapters suggest several powerful factors to build your students' brains. They include managing the cognitive load, developing better thinking skills, enhancing study skills and vocabulary, and building long-term, short-term,

117

and working memory. Every one of those is powerful, but using several will help create cognitive powerhouses.

Here's the big question: What mindset narrative do you have? See figure 13.1.

You Are Your Mindset: Which Is Yours?

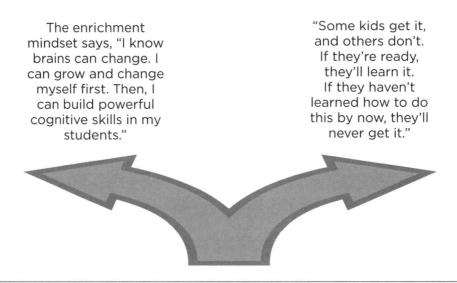

The enrichment mindset says, "I know brains can change. I can grow and change myself first. Then, I can build powerful cognitive skills in my students."

"Some kids get it, and others don't. If they're ready, they'll learn it. If they haven't learned how to do this by now, they'll never get it."

Figure 13.1: You are your mindset—the enrichment mindset.

Make this year the story of how you develop your students, as would a coach for his or her athletes. In this case, you'll develop the capacity to learn. Now, you have a choice to make: What will be your new alternative and more empowering narrative to explain failure and foster positive changes for the future?

Fill in the following blanks with your name and a strategy from this mindset. Repeat the phrase daily until it's automatic.

"I, _____, am committing to developing the enrichment mindset with my students every single day. I will begin with one of the strategies mentioned, which is _____. I will continue this until I have mastery and it's automatic. At that point, I'll learn something new to foster student success."

Reflection and Decision

All meaningful and lasting change starts with a mirror. Self-reflect first. How strong are your students' learn-to-learn skills? Your decision to grow the enrichment mindset in your students includes:

1. Choosing a new narrative about your students and yourself that includes the enrichment mindset

2. Using one of the strategies in the preceding chapters to develop cognitive skills with a fierce urgency

3. Creating a support process to ensure successful implementation

That support process may include any of the following: engaging colleagues, sending notes to yourself, and creating lesson plans that include fresh strategies and narratives.

Quick Consolidation

At school, I often hear teachers describe "low" students. But their brains are only responding to environmental input. Since the brain can change, there are no low students, only students in low environments. As educators, we get students for nine hundred hours a year and often spend more time with them than their parents. We can change the brains of the next generation to help it succeed.

Students with a growth mindset might say, "I can change and grow and learn from my mistakes." The growth mindset means that failures are an opportunity to learn from mistakes and get better. It affirms the value of effort, attitude, and improved strategy. It does not claim that everyone can become an Einstein; merely that everyone has potential for growth. The enrichment mindset can become a different way you think about students from now on. Everything can be enriched: social skills, punctuality, respect, vocabulary, and, of course, cognitive skills. This is an amazing moment in your life when the burden of low expectations is suddenly invalid. You now know that all students really can learn, as long as you are an ally.

The power of engaging the growth mindset is huge. Once you begin to say, "What else can I enrich?" a whole new world of teaching opens up for you. You can measure the strength of your enrichment mindset, not just in what you say to your students but also in what you teach them. That process speaks volumes and shows your students you believe in their potential. So, while it is fresh on your mind, start thinking of some higher goals for your students to reach this year (or semester).

PART THREE

WHY THE GRADUATION MINDSET?

CHAPTER 14

SECRETS OF THE GRADUATION MINDSET

This chapter begins with my own personal mission for college and career readiness standards. I am committed to helping 100 percent of K–12 students graduate job or college ready. When I share this mission with others, some feel like kindred spirits and like my gutsy goal. But others simply smile, and I suspect they silently say to themselves, "Right; like *that's* going to happen." But who on your staff would say that? Are you a teacher who subscribes to the deficit model, which suggests that the poor will always struggle because they are "broken"? Actually, anyone who thinks that way should know the facts. High-poverty schools can and do succeed. It is often the staff's mindset that is broken.

The Graduation Mindset

Let's review what you are up against. Every day, when you go to work, remind yourself, "Our students need every minute I can invest in each and every day." In this book, I have shared scientific research showing that brains can change and strategies to help your students succeed. Yes, it's hard work, and you should know that up front. Without focus, the amount of distracting noise out there can make you, and students, feel crazy. Tune it out. Stop listening to the negativity. Fill your mind with the dreams that you and your students have for success. You can make the choice to do it. We are all counting on you to manage that noise and help students manage it too. See figure 14.1 (page 124).

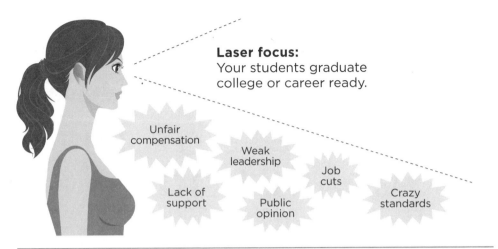

Figure 14.1: Learning to manage the noise.

Before you can understand the thinking of a teacher with the graduation mindset, it helps to contrast it with the opposite mindset. Teachers who struggle in this area may say something like one or more of the following statements. Ask yourself if you have occasionally heard these comments at school.

- "Graduation would be nice, but most of these students don't even try."
- "I'm a positive person, but realistically, these students have come from pretty bad environments."
- "The parents don't even care. Heck, most of them only have one parent at home. Why should I care?"
- "These students are often tardy, truant, or absent. They may have it rough at home, but still, most don't participate in class. I don't think they even want to graduate."

When you see these comments in writing, they're pretty depressing, aren't they? As you read these, ask yourself if you'd like your own son or daughter to attend this school. Now, in contrast, the bold, charge-ahead graduation mindset of those who help students become college and career ready is *much* different. The graduation mindset says, "Focus on what matters. Be an ally to help students graduate college and career ready."

> The graduation mindset says, "Focus on
> what matters. Be an ally to help students
> graduate college and career ready."

I am happy to share a few statements I have heard when visiting high-performing schools.

- "I choose to work here because I love changing lives. I give my own students the skills, knowledge, and hope that each needs to graduate and succeed in this world."

- "I like my job. Graduation is our first priority. What makes my day is when I help a student succeed who was failing before. Now, that's priceless."

- "At our school, every teacher is totally committed to helping students succeed. In fact, I would go so far as to say, 'We simply won't let them fail.'"

A Hard Look at the Evidence

Successful schools do anything and everything that is needed. Hundreds (maybe thousands) of high-poverty schools succeed every year (out of tens of thousands possible). One researcher estimated that there were 3,592 high-performing, high-poverty schools in the year 2000 (Jerald, 2001); but others assert that the number is far lower (Krashen, 2002). Several things are problematic: most of the research is well over a decade old, researchers disagree on the standard to which schools should be held, and finally, a high-performing school may lose its coveted status when new leadership arrives with a lesser skill set, lower expectations, or without a mission-driven philosophy. What is important for you to know is that there are schools (that's plural, not just one) that are high poverty, high minority, and high performing. If there was only one school in the country, you could dismiss it as an outlier. But once we see many schools succeeding, the case for it being impossible disappears. I always ask the staff at a school, "How many success stories do you need?"

High-performing schools do things differently; that's why they succeed. The difference has nothing to do with broken students and more to do with broken spirits among the staff. When I share the stories of successful teachers or schools, some teachers are awed and want to be like them.

Others see those teachers as a statistical exception. They ask, "Yes, but was it in our city? Yes, but was it a public school? Yes, but do they have the same ethnicity as our school? Yes, but did they have the same job losses we just did? Yes, but do they have the same budget problems we have?" Of course, none of those questions really matter. Even one successful public school confirms that it can be done—and there are many, many schools succeeding.

The high-performing school staff don't make excuses, nor do they talk about the schools that fail. They roll up their sleeves and go to work. You should know there are schools that have done crazy, nearly impossible things to help students graduate. It does take very high intention. I mean this; schools with high poverty and test scores show it is possible. The Education Trust's Dispelling the Myth (https://edtrust.org/dispelling _the_myth) recognizes low-income schools that are high achieving. Among secondary schools, here are two quick examples. In San Diego, 95 percent of the students at the Preuss School are from poverty, yet it is ranked in the top 100 schools in the United States, where 97 percent of students graduate (U.S. News & World Report, 2016). In Chicago, consider Urban Prep Academies: 100 percent of high school graduates were accepted to college (Urban Prep Academies, 2016).

What do high-performing schools do? Here is the policy analysis from the Center for Public Education (2005). There are five major building blocks.

1. A culture of high expectations and caring for students
2. A safe and positively disciplined environment
3. A strong instructional school leader
4. Hard-working, committed, and able teachers
5. A curriculum focused on academic achievement that emphasizes basic skills in mathematics and literacy

There are also five core practices.

1. Protected instructional time
2. Ongoing, actionable, and diagnostic assessment
3. Parents as partners in learning
4. Professional development to improve student achievement
5. Strong collaboration among teachers and staff

Now, what do classroom teachers do to make this happen? Here are examples of just a few of the strategies that high-performing schools use.

- Upper-grade students mentoring lower-grade students (for example, eleventh and twelfth graders mentoring ninth and tenth graders, and fourth and fifth graders sharing college options and job options with first and second graders)
- Partnerships with a local university to supply no-cost tutors to support student learning in one-hour homework sessions after school
- Strong arts and physical education programs that develop life skills, self-discipline, and teamwork
- School-to-job programs that help students find relevancy in their time at high school (for example, working in the cafeteria as part of a culinary arts program, learning to repair A/C and heating units as

well as drywall and paint, or learning business skills by running the student store)

- After-school programs that help students make important social and business contacts in the community with one-hour question-and-answer sessions with local businesspeople, community leaders, and counselors

- Ninth-grade scholarship committee to help students navigate the process of preparing high school coursework and scholarship applications

How did you respond to this list? Did you think, "Those sound good," then just keep reading? High-poverty, high-performing schools consider every option. They hold discussions, look at their data, listen to students via student surveys, and are fanatic about patching any gaps that hurt students' chances for graduation. The preceding items are solid-gold ideas that can transform your school. Please circle them, tag this page, and talk about them at your school. The following two chapters offer strategies to help your students prepare for graduation—no matter what grade they're in. These strategies include the following.

1. Support alternative solutions.
2. Prepare for college and careers.

Quick Consolidation

In the following chapters, you'll begin a new narrative, one all about reaching a school goal of 100 percent graduation. Remember, the graduation mindset says, "Focus on what matters. Be an ally to help students graduate college and career ready." When this is your mindset, heaven and earth will move for you. Why? Your intention is clear, and your attention to the goal is focused and strong. You have the skills, and the outcome can become real.

CHAPTER 15

SUPPORT ALTERNATIVE SOLUTIONS

Let's start with a simple question: If you knew of a program that kept students in school, reduced student discipline problems, strengthened cognitive capacity, reduced dropouts, and improved graduation rates, would you support it? Of course you would!

Why did I ask you this question?

Researchers have studied programs that do those things for decades and yet, we have to beg, plead, fight, and scream for their implementation. Across the United States, fewer and fewer schools include arts programs and physical fitness programs. For arts, over 40 percent of secondary schools do not require coursework in arts for graduation (Parsad & Spiegelman, 2012). Seven in ten parents say their child's school has zero physical education (NPR, Robert Wood Johnson Foundation, & Harvard School of Public Health, 2013). Somehow, other new curricula with far less evidence to support their contribution to student achievement seem to push them out of the public eye.

This chapter reviews two strong ways to keep students in school and help them graduate college or career ready. The alternatives that help students soar are: (1) arts and (2) physical activity. Before you say, "Yeah, yeah, yeah. I've heard that a million times," let's review why these alternatives should be a part of your school. It's OK to have opinions; we all have them. But in the process of education, every dollar spent is being scrutinized. That means, if a parent or teacher asks, "Can you show me if this is worth the dollars or time we are investing for our students?" I want to be able to say, "Yes!" Because if you are fighting for students to graduate college or career ready, these top the list of high-return investments.

Why Support the Arts?

First, let's review the arts research. A major study shows that students who underwent thirty-six weeks of musical training showed a reliable increase in IQ (Schellenberg, 2004). Musical training enhances memory (Ho, Cheung, & Chan, 2003), academic achievement (Southgate & Roscigno, 2009), and social development (Catterall, 2003). Maybe most critically, a U.S. longitudinal aggregate of four databases with thousands of low–socioeconomic status students found clear positive differences (Catterall, 2009). The students had higher graduation rates, fewer discipline issues, and better grades.

Low-income students receiving the top fifth in arts time available were compared to those in the bottom quintile (Catterall, Dumais, & Hampden-Thompson, 2012). The results were clear: members of the top quintile group were more likely to graduate from high school, get an associate's degree or bachelor's degree, and earn mostly As in college. They were more likely to have higher scores in writing, science, and mathematics in high school as well as to participate in extracurricular activities. They were more likely to read a newspaper, get involved in student government, and volunteer in their community. This is dramatic evidence of the value of arts for students from poverty. The study concludes that low–socioeconomic status students with strong arts experience achieve as much as those in the general population (Catterall et al., 2012).

In the following sections, you'll learn how arts build what I call the academic operating system and how to use the arts more in the classroom.

How Arts Build the Academic Operating System

Here we define arts as the big four: musical arts (playing an instrument), performing arts (theater, choir, dance, tap dance, and comedy), kinetic arts (sculpture), and visual arts (drawing, painting, and so on). There are school success factors that I call our *academic operating system*. These are brain systems that are developed in precise and lasting ways from long-term exposure to arts. Students are more likely to be successful when they excel at these skills (Skoe & Kraus, 2012). Among them, I include the following (see figure 15.1).

Having said that, we will focus on the musical arts and physical activity. Simply put, the evidence is strongest for student growth among those two. As you can see in figure 15.1, the process of participating in typical arts activities (music, dance, visual arts, and so on) is a clear brain builder.

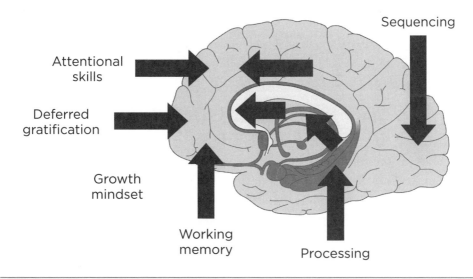

Figure 15.1: How arts build the academic operating system.

In my experience, the arts influence the following five factors when students participate in them three to five days a week for at least thirty to ninety minutes at a time.

1. **Effort:** Motivation and the ability to defer gratification
2. **Processing skills:** Auditory, visual, and tactile
3. **Attentional skills:** Engage, focus, and disengage as needed
4. **Memory capacity:** Short-term and working memory
5. **Sequencing skills:** Knowing the order of a process

In addition to these five factors, arts support the graduation mindset. Schools that
have music programs have significantly higher attendance rates than do those without
programs (93.3 percent as compared to 84.9 percent) and have significantly higher graduation rates than do those without music programs (90.2 percent as compared to 72.9
percent). In addition, those that rate their programs as "excellent or very good" have an
even higher graduation rate (90.9 percent; Nagel, 2006).

There are multiple ways you can engage arts in the classroom. Use arts yourself and,
ideally, please use a qualified arts teacher if possible. Your ideal strategy is to have a cer-
tified arts teacher work with your students for fifteen to thirty minutes for three days a
week at both the elementary and secondary level. When there are not enough art teachers, teachers can use arts in their own way (drawings, gestures, dance, and energizers).

How important are the arts? In a U.S. study of twenty-five thousand secondary school
students over four years, the researchers found significant correlations between high
involvement in arts learning and general academic success (Catterall, Chapleau, &
Iwanaga, 1999). But in a follow-up on the same students at age twenty-five, the results

were striking. More of the low-income students were in college and had better grades, and were more likely to have an advanced degree and be employed in the future. They were also more likely to vote and be involved in volunteer work (Catterall, 2009). It is clear that the arts impact the graduation mindset.

How to Use More Musical Arts and Physical Activity in the Classroom

For musical arts, if you allow students to learn and use an instrument, their skill sets will improve. Music instruction helps students learn to read (Standley, 2008). Three or more years of instrumental music training enhance auditory discrimination, fine motor skills, vocabulary, and nonverbal reasoning (Forgeard, Winner, Norton, & Schlaug, 2008). Music students have much better verbal memory than those without it, and the longer the training, the better the verbal memory (Ho et al., 2003).

Maybe the quickest way for students to get music training (without a music instructor) is by learning to play on an iPad. Consider the use of these apps: Tiny Piano, Nota, 50in1 Piano HD, Musical Touch, Pro Keys, and Twelve One. These will get a student hooked on being a musician! There are many YouTube videos that teach introductory music lessons. That's not as good as a qualified music teacher, but it is better than no music exposure at all.

Playing a musical instrument involves the synchronization of many different, demanding tasks. The resulting coordination of mental activity not only spurs structural growth in the brain but also gives musicians an edge in perception, which spills over into the realms of language and spatial relations. Because of this overlap, musicians repeatedly outperform their nonmusical peers on tests of IQ, verbal memory, reading skills, creative problem solving, geometry, and number systems (Catterall et al., 2012).

Surprisingly, music lessons bring a socioemotional advantage too as young musicians are more able to detect emotional nuances in speech, enjoy higher self-esteem, and are more likely to exhibit productive characteristics such as cooperation, motivation, responsibility, and initiative. These many advantages, which research shows to hold up across cultures, appear to be independent of genetic or socioeconomic advantage and are especially striking in students who start early, practice often, and keep the skills over time (Catterall et al., 2012).

To support drama, allow students to role-play a topic. Students can do this in science (for example, to show how an experiment will work, a reaction of chemicals, or an ecological outcome). They can do it in mathematics (for example, to show a key formula, how each part of an equation plays out, or a memorable way to store the formula), or in English (for example, to tell a story, explain a review, or show relevance to student lives). Performing and learning the skills of drama will build a large group of transferrable skills. Movement, often part of drama, can affect cognition in many ways. In figure 15.2, you'll see the connection between motor skills and academic skills.

Academic Skills

Wire the
Brain for
Academic
Success

Reading	Mathematics	Written or Oral Language	General Knowledge
Associative thinking	Deductive thinking	Abstract thinking	Inductive thinking
Sequencing	Analysis	Sequence synthesis	Organizing
Visualization	Patterning visual discrimination	Verbal ability	Memory and reasoning
Center line skills	Eye-foot coordination	Spatial coordination	Hand-eye and hand-foot tracking
Dynamic Balance	**Body Awareness**	**Unilateral, Bilateral, Crosslateral Balance**	**Locomotor Skills**

Motor Skills

Figure 15.2: Wiring the brain for success.

Now, let's visit a pro-arts teacher to find out how much the arts matter (Esquith, 2007).

An upper-elementary teacher in South Los Angeles, California, taught at a high-poverty elementary school. The neighborhood was known more for crime and non–English speakers than anything else. Over 70 percent of his students were from poverty, and most were second language learners. If you track the students from his entire elementary school, only 32 percent graduate from high school. But if you track the students from his fifth-grade class only, 100 percent graduate and go on to college. The primary vehicle for his students' success is the arts.

The students dance, learn how to play an instrument, and perform the Shakespearean play *As You Like It*. The next time you think you can't make a difference, go to YouTube and type in "The Hobart Shakespeareans," and see his students perform. The arts are a huge difference maker, and they change the brain in positive ways (Asbury & Rich, 2008).

Why Support Physical Activity?

Let's revisit the value of physical activity. In a longitudinal study of over eighty-three thousand New York City middle school students enrolled between 2006–2007 and 2011–2012, there was a substantial correlation between fitness from the previous year and a greater improvement in academic ranking (the average was over 20 percentile points compared to other unfit students). The testing used was a composite percentile based on yearly state standardized mathematics and English language arts test scores (Bezold et al., 2014). Another study finds that vocabulary learning is 20 percent faster after intense physical exercise (Winter et al., 2007). In California, using data from almost a million students, researchers find physical education is also associated with enhanced reading and mathematics scores (Grissom, 2005). See figure 15.3.

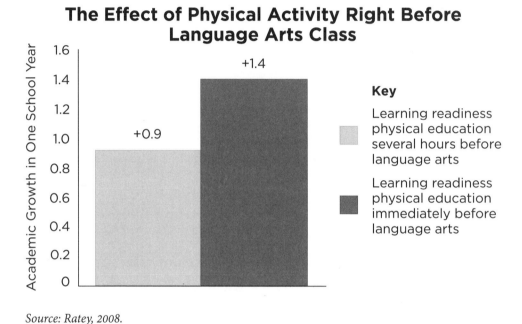

Source: Ratey, 2008.

Figure 15.3: Physical activity fosters literacy skills.

For many students, mathematics is a tough, gritty subject. But physical activity boosts dopamine, which fosters increased effort, optimism, and working memory (all of which can help students perform better in mathematics). It also raises the production of noradrenaline, which improves focus and long-term memory. In Naperville, Illinois, researchers found that physical activity supports positive growth in algebra scores (Illinois Public Health Institute, 2013). See figure 15.4.

Many schools struggle as a whole with classroom discipline. But physical activity, in multiple tests, has been shown to reduce classroom discipline issues (Ratey, 2008). See figure 15.5 for the influence of a daily fitness program (PE4life).

Another study shows boosts in self-confidence (Carlson et al., 2008) due to physical activity. More studies show exercise supports students' executive functioning skills, including attention (Best, 2010; Budde, Voelcker-Rehage, Pietrabyk-Kendziorra, Ribeiro, & Tidow, 2008). A key part of physical activity is *the capture*. I call it the capture because

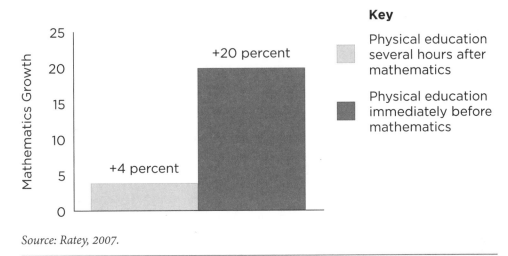

Source: Ratey, 2007.

Figure 15.4: Physical activity fosters mathematics skills.

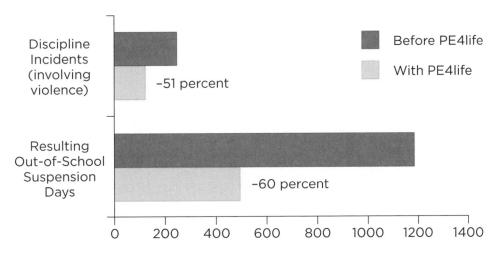

Source: Ratey, 2007.

Figure 15.5: Physical activity reduces discipline problems.

there are few things in life that you can genuinely get real control over to lower stress and succeed. Moving your body is one of those gems. This is right at the heart of the graduation mindset. Physical activity is one of the best ways to feel more in control of your own body and your life.

There are multiple ways you can engage physical activity in the classroom.

How Physical Activity Fosters New Brain Cells

The human brain can and does produce new brain cells, but chronic stress and poor nutrition decrease the new cell production, which increases the chance for depression. A third of students from poverty suffer from chronic stress and depression (Pratt & Brody, 2014). However, there is increasing evidence that voluntary gross motor exercise is a viable preventive and treatment strategy for depression (Yau, Li, Xu, & So, 2015). In one study, young homeless mothers with a history of depression and anxiety took a thirty-minute dance program that enhanced mindfulness twice a week for eight weeks. The dance training improved more than aerobic fitness; it decreased their symptoms of depression and anxiety (Shors, Olson, Bates, Selby, & Alderman, 2014).

New brain cells contribute to better mood, memory, weight management, and cognition (Marin-Burgin & Schinder, 2012; van Praag, Fleshner, Schwartz, & Mattson, 2014). We can improve neurogenesis (the production of new brain cells) with voluntary gross motor activity (Pereira et al., 2007).

Figure 15.6 shows the results of animal research indicating a doubling of new brain cells for rats that were given running wheels compared with those without the exercise option (Brown et al., 2003). Studies on humans have verified this effect (Erickson et al., 2011).

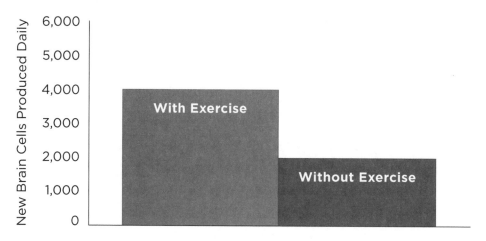

Source: Brown et al., 2003.

Figure 15.6: Exercise fosters new brain cells.

Finally, a long-term study shows the connection between fitness and cognition (London & Castrechini, 2011). This study finds that overall physical fitness is a strong predictor of academic achievement, and the lack of fitness begins as early as fourth grade. Another study of over seventeen hundred students finds that sixth- and ninth-grade students with superior fitness score significantly better on mathematics and social studies tests compared with less fit students (Coe, Peterson, Blair, Schutten, & Peddie, 2013).

How to Use Physical Activity in the Classroom

In any way you can, support a full twenty- to thirty-minute physical activity break at the K–5 level. Do not, under any circumstances, punish a student by keeping him or her in the classroom during recess. There are dozens of alternatives (for example, stand last in line for lunch, lose privileges, stay after school for five minutes for reflective writing, and so on). You could also keep students more engaged to reduce behavioral issues and teach students the behaviors you want, rather than only punishing bad behavior.

For example, are you giving students constant stretch breaks and energizers to burn off energy? If not, include out-of-seat activities every ten to twenty minutes during your class. Take students outside, and let them do laps around a fitness or walking area. One K–5 teacher took students out on the field and did a power walk for a full lap with her class. Soon, other teachers got in on the practice, and campuswide excitement began to grow about daily ten-minute power walks and the value of physical activity. Help get the brain ready to reason by keeping it healthy and in top physical shape.

A great way to support physical activity in your classroom is to form teams for energizers that get the body moving. Assign a personal trainer to keep each team (four per team for grades K–5 and five per team for 6–12) engaged in the activity. Give personal trainers a cue every fifteen to twenty-five minutes to get the team moving, and rotate the trainers every two weeks. Try the following activities with your class.

- Invite students to run in place for one minute. Once you begin, students will get excited, especially if you encourage some friendly competition or collaboration. Students who are extra active, bored, or just need to release a little steam will find this is a jewel.

- Integrate movement with subject areas. For example, check out activities at Action Based Learning (http://actionbasedlearning.3dcartstores.com).

- Do whole-group activities that bring everyone together. For example, allow a student to teach the class a dance step.

- Allow student volunteers to be leaders. Everyone follows as he or she walks, marches, and dances around the classroom for forty-five seconds.

- Play an imaginary sport. Students within a team all stand up, and each picks a favorite sport. One at a time, that person goes through the kinesthetic motions of that sport, while the other team members mimic the motions for thirty seconds. Rotate to the next team member, and everyone follows that student too. This is great fun and goes quickly.

At the secondary level, students still need to move their bodies. This means physical education is critical, but so are classroom activities that allow students to move.

Quick Consolidation

This chapter was all about alternative ideas—the arts and physical education. The graduation mindset casts a wide net across the landscape and says, "Let's leave no stone unturned."

Enrich every student, every day to move him or her toward graduation. Graduation is not an accident; it is a hard, long-term process that takes its toll on students. When you provide the tools, hope, and relationships and go above and beyond, the students will feel it. They will feel that graduation is indeed that important. Once they are on board, success belongs to everybody. Can I count on you?

CHAPTER 16

PREPARE FOR COLLEGE AND CAREERS

There have always been some students who struggle or fail in nearly every area of school until they get to do something with their hands, participate in something physical, or get outdoors and learn. Some students practically live for these activities that may include vocational training, outdoor learning, project-based work, field trips, apprentice learning, and service learning. As a generalization, keep your younger students closer to school. The novelty of outside experiences is more likely to overwhelm third-grade students, depending on their previous at-home experiences. They'll remember the field trip but will likely learn less from it than if you just use a simple outdoor science activity within the school grounds.

The Power of Career and Technical Education

Let's explore some of the strategies from high-performing schools I have worked with. These are from highly successful schools that discovered how to make the magic happen.

- **Increase exposure:** Help all students get exposure to college and jobs. Have all fifth graders partner up. They pick one college and research it well (costs, scholarships, areas of specialization, location, demographics, and so on). Then, they prepare a fifteen-minute poster session to share with second graders. All fourth graders do the same with a career that only needs a high school degree.

- **Link behaviors and outcomes:** Help students link current behaviors and outcomes with a goal. "Your extra time on the homework really paid off. That effort will help you get into the college you want."

- **Link the content:** Use classroom content areas to talk about professions. For example, for high school science, media arts, language, or mathematics classes, mention jobs that require mastery of these subjects (biologist, graphic designer, translator, and engineer). Keep sharing the occupations that tie into the class you teach.

- **Assume the attribution:** Use the "when" phrase, not the "if" phrase. Instead of "If you graduate," say "When you graduate." Instead of "If you go to college," say "When you go to college."

- **Boost system knowledge:** Ensure that all students in high school, starting at the ninth-grade level, get a personalized scholarship committee. This group may comprise three to four counselors, teachers, or office staff. The role of this committee is to assess the student's interests, find schools that are strong in these areas, discover the entry requirements (such as grades and classes), find scholarship pathways, and help him or her make a plan to take the classes, get the grades, and earn a scholarship.

- **Offer supplemental programs:** Is your secondary school really committed to student success? Consider the following secondary strategies.

  - Provides a daily forty-five-minute after-school session with tutors from a nearby university (at zero cost to the school) to ensure that every student gets 100 percent of assigned homework done right

  - Offers a strong mentorship program for all new students

  - Provides language translation opportunities for families

  - Raises money to ensure students have the transportation they need

  - Has all students take honors classes (through the AVID program; Advancement Via Individual Determination)

  - Has no academic tracking system due to AVID

- Requires all students starting in seventh grade to participate in a schoolwide exhibition and the school science fair
- Provides college-level workshops for parents to involve them in supporting their students in the college journey

By the way, this 100 percent–poverty public school sends over 90 percent of its students to college. It raises students' expectations and goals, and then delivers the support to help students make their goals happen.

Help find ways to promote career and technical education at your school. Provide mentors, since we know the research supports this action step (Chan et al., 2013). There are thousands of jobs waiting for skilled workers, but we have not prepared students for them. Here are some jobs for which we should be offering skill sets.

- Computer coding and software development
- Industrial services (welding, construction, and plumbing)
- Audio and video technology, information technology support, and electronic data processing (systems operations)
- Food and nutrition science, culinary arts
- Business development and marketing
- Agricultural development
- Animal production, science, and business
- Hospitality and tourism
- Plant science, natural resources, and ecology
- Corrections, law enforcement, and security

How can you offer these? Foster career and technical education programs within the school, not just as an after-graduation choice. Ron Fitzgerald understood this problem. In 1971, he pioneered one of the most successful career and technical education programs in the United States. The school, Minuteman High School (http://minuteman. org) in Lexington, Massachusetts, was filled with many districtwide transfer students who were considered discipline issues (the "bad behavior" kids) and needed something different.

Once in his school, students realized that their three biggest complaints about school were reversed. First, every teacher cared a great deal about them and their future. Second, although every student had classes to take, every student also had things to do (they were fully physically engaged every day). Third, classes were highly relevant—they received

100 percent career preparation. In short, the school met students' biggest needs: care about me, engage me, and make it relevant.

These students became productive and many graduated (88 percent) because much of the school curriculum fostered job skills that created instant relevancy. The school developed job skills in many areas. For example, the cafeteria had a culinary arts program for work in the hospitality industry. The custodian provided jobs around the campus as part of job training for heating, electrical, painting, air conditioning, and drywall repair. The student store provided workplace options for students interested in entrepreneurship skills. When I walked around the campus in 2002, I saw energy, focus, and purpose in the students' body language. They *wanted* to be in school. Although they were supposedly the problem students, they all looked pretty good to me.

As of 2016, Massachusetts has a network of twenty-six academically rigorous vocational-technical high schools serving twenty-seven thousand students. Students take traditional academic courses but spend half their time apprenticing in a field of their choice. These include computer repair, telecommunications networking, carpentry, early childhood education, plumbing, heating, refrigeration, and cosmetology.

Amazingly, these schools have some of the state's highest graduation and college matriculation rates, and close to 96 percent pass the state's rigorous high-stakes graduation test. Fitzgerald's school was the original model for this job-driven success story. Long after Fitzgerald retired, the rest of the state is discovering what he did well. Massachusetts is increasing Minuteman's programs across the state.

Here are three options for a program like that of Minuteman High School that you might implement in your school.

1. Contact your state department of education for more information on what is available for blending career and technical education into your school.

2. Start slow and implement one program a year.

3. Do miniprograms that take less time. The following are some suggestions for effective miniprograms at your school.

    - Students research and create a simulation for dealing with fire drills, bullying, hostage situations, or floods.

    - Students establish ties with local businesses for apprentice work.

    - Students develop field trips within the school to see staff, vegetation, or design elements.

    - Students set up a tour of a local business during slow times— such as weeks with no testing or holidays.

- Students form partnerships with Boy Scouts or Girl Scouts, 4-H club, or local camping facilities.

- Students work with local museums, cultural exhibits, and art galleries for field trips.

Although I am college educated, I don't feel that college is for everybody. Any time you push students too hard in any direction, you'll get resistance. Here are options for students who are not ready for college. Introduce them to the following resources.

- *Better Than College: How to Build a Successful Life Without a Four-Year Degree* by Blake Boles

- Zero Tuition College (www.ztcollege.com)

- *40 Alternatives to College* by James Altucher

- TED and TEDx Talks that make great introductions to careers (search through the education category)

The more options students see, the better the likelihood that they'll find the right fit. What else can you do to help students graduate career or college ready? The key here is to put yourself in your students' shoes. What will move them forward in life? What can you do immediately? How can you best facilitate the process?

- **College ready:** Do they have the life skills to deal with college life? Do they have solid study skills for each subject? Do they have a mentor to contact for support? If a student does not get a scholarship, here's what to do. Remind your students that college really can be free. The University of the People (http://uopeople.edu) is an accredited and tuition-free college (although there are some fees involved, such as $2,000 to $4,000 for tests).

- **Career ready:** Does every graduate have a resume? Does every graduate have interviewing skills through constant practice and feedback? Does each graduate have either a confirmed job or at least five leads to follow up on? Does he or she have a mentor to contact for support?

There are some great websites that may help students avoid uncertainty, stress, or confusion about the college process. Work with students on college help sites like the National Association for College Admission Counseling (www.nacacnet.org/studentinfo /Pages) and YouCanGo! (http://youcango.collegeboard.org). Remember, community colleges can be a great stepping stone to either a job or a four-year degree elsewhere.

Quick Consolidation

This chapter was all about the graduation mindset. This is a powerful mindset that says, "We will do whatever is necessary to help students graduate." Here we explored the career and technical education options. We visited a school, which had students who were sent as so-called discipline problems or even "bad boys." However, the principal understood that students simply wanted a school that gave them the only things they really cared about—relationships with caring teachers, relevant curriculum, and engaging classes. That's all the students wanted. When the school welcomed these elements, discipline problems vaporized, dreams were built, and graduation became real. This is what it takes at your school too. Can you take a step today toward that happening?

CHAPTER 17

LOCK IN THE GRADUATION MINDSET

The graduation mindset reminds you to use a filter in your work: "Is what I am doing *right now* moving this student toward graduation (and to be job or college ready)?" Highly effective teachers influence the narrative (their story), both in their students' lives and their own. The narrative is the predicted story about how things will turn out. Every time you get frustrated, get angry, or are tempted to back off, just pause. We all do these things.

Remind yourself that you are your students' best hope for a chance of success in life. Without you, many will not succeed. Your students need you at your best. You do not need to be perfect; just bring your best every day. That's the graduation mindset. Learn to focus on the rewards of your job. Nobody is going to triple your pay overnight, but you can have a far more rewarding job if you focus on the *why*.

Change the Narrative, Change Your Teaching

Which mindset narrative do you have? See figure 17.1 (page 146). Remember, you choose not what happens to you but how you respond to what happens to you. DNA is not your destiny. Circumstances are not your destiny. Right now I invite you to choose the narrative of every single student as a graduate: job or college ready. This year could be all about how you create great mindsets in which every student learns and succeeds.

You Are Your Mindset: Which Is Yours?

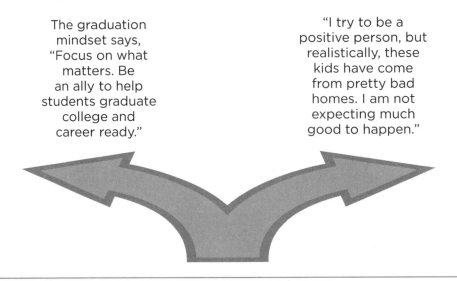

The graduation mindset says, "Focus on what matters. Be an ally to help students graduate college and career ready."

"I try to be a positive person, but realistically, these kids have come from pretty bad homes. I am not expecting much good to happen."

Figure 17.1: You are your mindset—the graduation mindset.

Fill in the following blanks with your name and a strategy from this mindset. Repeat the phrase daily until it's automatic.

"I, _____, am committing to developing the graduation mindset with my students every single day. I will begin with one of the strategies mentioned, which is _____. I will continue this until I have mastery and it's automatic. At that point, I'll learn something new to foster student success."

Reflection and Decision

No one is telling you this is easy. You are in a tough profession. All you can ask of yourself is to be true to yourself and your students. At any point in your work, if you're uncommitted and on the fence, your students will sense it. If you're just waiting for retirement, how many students will you adversely influence before you call it quits? Your students need a teacher who is all in.

You *always* have choices, and they arise from your mindsets. You can choose to change jobs, addresses, friends, and attitudes so that you love your job. But any ambivalence will hurt your students. This is a new narrative for most. It is the habit of purposeful planning on a daily basis. Yes, you can do it. And, yes, it's true, inch by inch, it's a cinch.

Quick Consolidation

Be positive, build cognitive capacity, and own the graduation mentality. In classrooms, be the teacher who is confident and decisive, knowing the future may be uncertain, but it will be good. There is typically a sense of community among students and the teacher as they work toward a common goal. Focus on what matters: be an ally to help students graduate job or college ready. A teacher from a high-performing, high-poverty school emailed me once to thank me for including her school in my book, *Teaching With Poverty in Mind*. In her school, 100 percent of the students are from poverty, yet over 95 percent every year go to college. Why does her school succeed? "Our school simply won't let you fail," she said (M. Olivas, personal communication, October 11, 2011). Take a moment, and let that sink in.

If you're still just a bit unsure of what strategies are right to use, go ahead and turn to the appendices when you finish this chapter.

Appendix A
Rich Lesson Planning

Rich lesson planning is critical. When your lesson plans are rich, they include *how* you teach, not just *what* to teach. For example, in a lesson plan, you might write a note to yourself, "Be sure to ensure students make their own decisions on this—give them control!" or, your lesson plan says, "Stop complaining; build the skills they don't have!"

Let's be honest: planning is work. Fortunately, it will pay off, and I'll show you how. I use a secondary lesson plan, but you can easily adapt it to a K–5 unit. This chapter discusses the benefits of collaboration, preassessment, relevance and buy-in, and attribution when planning lessons.

Collaboration

To develop high-powered lesson plans, work together in groups that fit your needs; these may be grade-level teams or content-level teams. This collaborative process is the key to success because you'll be able to develop common goals, language, and process for success. After developing goals and objectives, the process works backward into the lesson to ensure all the pieces are in play to get the outcome you want. Multiple studies show the value of higher levels of teacher collaboration and peer learning (Johnson, 2010).

However, teacher collaboration guarantees nothing. Collaboration works only when staff members focus on doing the right things well and following a staff-established success pattern. Collaborating about the right things, sharing ideas, solving problems, and planning lessons all support student achievement. There needs to be a list of norms in the staff lounge of how your staff run their meetings as well as how they accomplish their goals. This is the time to focus on the goal and make every minute count in your meeting time.

Set lofty goals for mastery learning. To develop a love of learning, students will need to learn how to learn in satisfying ways. Some things in life require only shallow learning. When students learn an address or phone number for pizza delivery, it's shallow learning. But when it comes to classroom learning, we'd like deeper, mastery learning. That's where student satisfaction builds into a love of learning. Support this deeper learning through big goals, and students will begin to love school.

Foster big challenges from big goals, and you can get big results. First, match the big goals with the standards necessary for academic success. Big goals would be: help every student graduate college or career ready. Next, how do we do that? We meet or exceed the standards. Now, let's ensure we have content in our lesson plans that matches. That's what staff collaboration can help you do: match planning with the ultimate test objectives. Post your team's steps for turning school problems into actionable solutions so you can easily replicate your prior successes. Check out the following ten steps.

1. Look at the data.

2. Turn data into meaning.

3. Discuss concerns.

4. Break down the meaning into actionable work.

5. Make learning goals.

6. Turn the work into lesson plans.

7. Use quality feedback standards for all.

8. Establish implementation goals.

9. Use frequent feedback from coaches or school leaders.

10. Get feedback on instruction from colleagues or leaders watching your lesson.

Once you've finished planning, you're ready for the next step. Teaching is, of course, not a top-down profession. Teaching is a carefully orchestrated dance. You're the pro, and the student is the amateur. The first thing the pro does is figure out what skills and attitudes the amateur has. That is called the preassessment. Without it, you have no clue where to start.

Preassessment

Deeper learning builds on basic skills and knowledge to gain expertise. Before a unit of instruction, give your students a unit preassessment to determine their level of background knowledge on the standards. Or you can just give them a short-and-sweet assessment about a particular learning objective to determine what you need to teach before a lesson. You need to know which (if any) of the basic skills (or content) that your students already know before you begin planning. As long as you provide the resources, their brains love challenges, so let's plan for them!

Naturally, you will begin by looking at student data. The data should tell you your students' current academic progress and appropriate targets. Be sure to plan lessons with mastery as the benchmark, not proficiency or compliance. First, ask yourself, "What will students need to know about this standard? At what level of thinking do I want them to engage with that standard? And how will they show it so their learning is visible?" The lesson plans must be objective driven for deep understanding. The initial objectives will, of course, include vocabulary and the subtitles and titles for core labeling of understanding. These are your cognitive signposts for knowledge clustering. But there's more.

As an example, if students read a story, what would be the evidence that they understand it? Should they create an outline, write a summary, or complete a worksheet? That would constitute basic learning, not mastery. It's a good start, but you'll want more. Students should ultimately be able to create a personality profile of each character, make inferences about his or her decisions in the story, and then quote passages that support their claims. They should be able to talk about the plotlines, their value, and why the author chose them. They should be able to assess the substance, value, and significance of this particular literature (compared to similar stories).

In short, ensure that you include depth in your lesson planning. Students will need to be able to analyze information critically, develop explanations of the content, know alternative viewpoints, and explain concepts. They should understand the core relationships within the learning and perform related tasks such as writing about, building on, showing, or speaking about the learning (Mehta & Fine, 2012).

To develop the mastery level, you'll need to demonstrate the criteria for the goals and products that you want to see. This means student exhibits, objects, props, and student papers that show what the end product will look like. Show exemplars, provide a checklist of criteria, and explain the criteria line by line for a rubric. Describe the product's features. Then, ask students to summarize the key discriminating features of the end product to confirm their understanding. Now, our next priority is getting our students to care about the learning. Without this next section, most planning is wasted.

Relevance and Buy-In

There are two big reasons to ensure you have relevance and buy-in. Both are highly practical reasons. First, if the brain is not buying into what's offered, it won't save the learning; it is forgotten. Second, students view school through the relevance filter. They think, "Why should I care about this?" Unless you address this concern, your teaching time may be wasted. Be sure to plan on how to develop the motivational drive students will need to reach the mastery level. Consider the relevance for your students by reviewing your lesson through their eyes. For the K–5 level, ways to make lessons relevant might include:

- Helping the homeless or needy
- Making friends
- Creating a garden to grow food for a homeless center
- Interviewing the elderly or documenting lives
- Helping stray cats and dogs

For some at the secondary level, the relevance angle might be:

- Learning social justice in social studies or history (how to solve big problems)
- Helping others by teaching content to a lower grade level
- Focusing on using the driving essential questions (for ideas use McTighe and Wiggins [2013] *Essential Questions*)
- Helping underclass students learn about jobs or colleges
- Building a theme park ride and preparing for travel
- Learning to run a business or rebuilding a city in mathematics or science
- Building a mentorship program for underclass students
- Competing with another class or school on projects
- Connecting goals to success

Relevance and buy-in are powerful hooks to get students interested. But a powerful teacher keeps the foot on the gas pedal. Attribution is the next tool to ensure students get the maximum value out of every moment in class. You'll learn to make it a habit to give a reason *why* to nearly everything you do.

Attribution

Attribution is the linking of one thing to another, as in cause and effect. If you say, "You ran fast, Kelly," that is a descriptive statement and maybe a compliment. But if you said, "You ran fast, Kelly; did your change in diet seem to help?" That is a link (attribution) where you linked the result (running fast) to an earlier action (different nutrition plan).

In a classroom, you may say, "Eric, love your effort. That's the kind of effort that will get you higher-paid promotions once you get your first job." Now, the student understands the attribution: more effort might equal more money later on.

Remember the amazing power of attribution. You must continually remind students that their success is tied to what they have already done or what they will do (factors over which they have control, such as effort, study time, and the use of appropriate strategies) and not tied to genes, luck, or circumstance. A struggling student is likely to attribute his or her weakness to a perceived low IQ, and he or she may withdraw effort when the challenge is great. But if the student attributes his or her poor results to lack of effort, then he or she may actually do something about it (Dweck, 1999). On a visceral level, this particular attribution must help the student advance toward the goal of either college or vocation. Build this into your lesson plans and sprinkle as needed to foster effort. You can say, "Erika, I loved how you stayed with that term paper. That kind of effort and grit is going to help you graduate from college."

Students work harder at behaviorally relevant topics. Ask the students to consider projects from a list including social justice, a better neighborhood, better law enforcement, or less racism (Butler-Barnes, Williams, & Chavous, 2012). You'll need to get buy-in. This is key to helping students want to achieve deeper learning.

Now that we have rolled out the starters, collaboration, preassessment, relevance and buy-in, and attribution, it's time to start locking down our lesson plan. You might say to me, "Eric, that's a lot of work!" Yes, you are right. But once you have done this over and over, it will become embedded in your brain. Soon, you'll be doing all of this with no prompts at all. Your memory of it will be stronger, but also you will have the positive feedback of actually using it.

A Rich Lesson Plan in Action

Now let's get started. Table A.1 (page 154) offers a sample lesson plan for a secondary science class. Be sure to review what you have learned about your students before you complete your lesson plan. There may be some students who got extra attention this week. You will review students' information in their learning profiles from the school and previous teachers. Often, teachers see a specific need to connect better with certain students to understand why they might be struggling or to use a specific strategy that a colleague used successfully. I complete learning profiles at the start of each semester.

Table A.1: Middle School Science Lesson Plan

Planning Steps	Details
Before Class	
Collecting Student Data	• I have thirty-one students (fifteen boys; sixteen girls) in my ninth-grade science classroom. Ninety-two percent of them receive free and reduced meals. The data on my students from last year showed that 22 percent of my classroom achieved proficiency, 8 percent expert, and 70 percent basic. My gutsy goal is for 100 percent proficiency this semester. • I review students' information in their learning profiles, and what I need to do for this lesson. • Yesterday's exit passes showed that 75 percent of my students across class periods did not distinguish among facts, reasoned judgment based on findings, and speculation in a text. They were also unsure of what was valid or invalid information. • I created a plan for reteaching these concepts to those students in particular. I created extension activities for those who did master the concepts.
Planning the Lesson **Memory Recall Strategies (see chapter 12)**	• I focused on priming students for one to two weeks before starting the science writing. The written arguments emphasize *discipline-specific content*. We will introduce claims about a science topic or issue, acknowledge and distinguish the claims from alternate or opposing claims, and organize the reasons and evidence logically. • Next, I'll ask students to do a three-minute content retrieval activity to see what they recall. • Students will work with a partner I have chosen. (I have a student list of Lexile scores, and they have their own records.)

Creating a Positive Physical Environment	• Open windows and shades (if possible). • Create a word wall with rich adjectives for writing and the tier two words that my classroom is focusing on (see chapter 11). • Place anchor charts on the walls with the most important science concepts and the writing process. • Play upbeat music. • Make posters and bulletin boards visible with content and skills students need to learn. • Bring in plants. • Write positive messages on the walls.
First Minute of Class Time	
Building Relationships	• When students enter, I am always at the door with a smile and a handshake. I make sure to exude safety and excitement. • Students sit with their teams. Team leaders check on the attendance to get things started. Then, before the learning begins, each team member gets thirty seconds to check in and update others on the most important thing on their mind. Then, the team leader shares today's goals.
Core Class Time	
Getting Started	• Early in class, I ask students to do a three-minute content-retrieval activity to see what they recall from yesterday. They turn this in, and I'll look this over while they are working. • I introduce the class objectives from the Next Generation Science Standards and Common Core State Standards, including the evidence for learning or success criteria. **Physical Science (Eighth Grade)** • Objective: Students will be able to write an argumentative paper about their perspective on cryobiology (study of living things at very low temperatures). (MS-PS1-3)

continued on next page ⇨

Getting Started (continued)	• Explanation: They will read several articles and visit many websites to determine the pros and cons of cryobiology. Then, they will formulate their opinions about it and argue for or against using the criteria for argumentative writing. (WHST.6–8.1) Question: Should the cryobiology technique be used to preserve living things? I share relevance: "Students, you have to learn how to make a case for *anything* in life so you can be your own advocate (for a better grade, in the legal system, to get hired, and so on). Without it, you won't get a fair shake." • Today's hooks are that every student gets to pick a famous scientist from history (I have a list for them), and they will be that scientist while they are writing their argumentative piece. • I write out and share sample arguments focused on the science content in the following order. I list these writing criteria so that students can self-evaluate, and peers can give feedback too. Criteria from the Common Core State Standards in argumentative writing for middle school: • WHST.6–8.1a—Introduce claims about a topic or issue, acknowledge and distinguish the claims from alternate or opposing claims, and organize the reasons and evidence logically. • WHST.6–8.1b—Support claims with logical reasoning and relevant, accurate data and evidence that demonstrate an understanding of the topic or text, using credible sources. • WHST.6–8.1c—Use words, phrases, and clauses to create cohesion and clarify the relationships among claims, counterclaims, reasons, and evidence. • WHST.6–8.1d—Establish and maintain a formal style. • WHST.6–8.1e—Provide a concluding statement or section that follows from and supports the argument presented.

Creating First Drafts	• First, I use a quick hook strategy. Students use a blank template that I provide with the writing criteria listed so they can keep track of my posted example to see if I have included all the criteria. Now, they have a sense of how it is done. They evaluate my writing and give me feedback on what I need to improve. My examples are about a different topic so that I don't give away my perspective before they write. • Next, they write a rough draft in their own words using the content from the texts and in the format we have just learned. They will have a partner to exchange ideas with for this process. • Yesterday's exit pass reminded me that students were unsure of what was valid or invalid information. I will check their understanding of this concept and form a small group of students to guide and reteach this concept with the science topic. • I will use this time to walk around and support the writing process, as well as to work with a small group of students who still need help with writing using the specific criteria.
Editing Time in Peer Group	• Next, students go back to their teams for editing again. They support each other and cooperatively work together to learn. Each team has a name, chant or song with special movements, and a different leader each week. They get points for proper behavior, teamwork, homework completion, celebrations, and other tasks. Each team will peer edit other team members' rough drafts. For homework, they will rewrite, using the peer comments for guidance. This feedback is critical.
Connecting to the Real World	• I will share a personal story about how I learned to write and how I learned to respond to feedback with the growth mindset. • During my connection time at the end of each class, I review the day's objectives and how they personally related to each student and the community.

continued on next page ⇨

Last Four Minutes of Class Time	
Strengthening Memory and Closing the Day	Using an exit pass, I have students answer the following questions. • What did you do well in your science writing summary? • What was the single most important change you had to make in your paper? Once they're finished, I put on music as students leave and thank them at the door.

Source: National Governors Association Center for Best Practices & Council of Chief State School Officers, 2010; NGSS Lead States, 2013.

*Visit **go.SolutionTree.com/instruction** for a reproducible version of this table.*

Many schools have district sites for developing lesson plans online. If you already have a site for it, use it. If not, visit 10 Minute Lesson Plans (www.10minutelessonplans.com). This free site will help you learn to create effective lesson plans in just a few minutes.

Notice the lesson plan in table A.1 uses strategies from this book. Not a bad start for a single class lesson. Of course, once you have taught a lesson using the strategies in this book, you'll start feeling more comfortable with them. You'll be ready for a couple of new strategies over time. As you become a lifelong learner, your comfort with change will keep rising. Because of this, your students will do well too. Don't forget that there are countless ways to accomplish the same objective. You can use the tools in this book in ways that would make a lesson seem completely different. But the core elements are the same. Here's a true example from a high-performing secondary mathematics teacher whose students typically progressed two to three years for each year he taught (Soloveichik, 1979).

Before we begin, remember there is far more academic support for structured, guided lessons than unguided learning in the classroom (Kirschner, Sweller, & Clark, 2006). Here's an example of structure and choice blended in a high-performing secondary mathematics class. Victor (who is now retired) was one of the most successful mathematics teachers (based on student year-on-year progress) who ever taught (Soloveichik, 1979). We'll look at the steps he took before and during class.

Before Class

For each class Victor created a one-page graphic outline of reference signals (arrows, stars, and cartoons), key ideas, concise conclusions, and selected extracts of schemas and examples plus connecting arrows, which show relationships between ideas. He gave this key working document to each student to start the semester. The mind map in figure A.1 (page 159) is similar to Victor's.

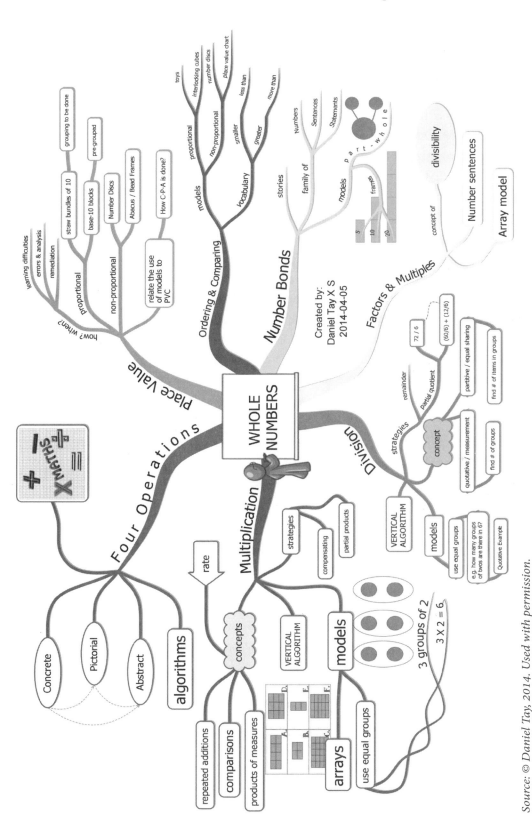

Source: © Daniel Tay, 2014. Used with permission.

Figure A.1: Mind map for whole numbers.

During Class

For daily accountability, Victor asked each student to write out a key understanding from the previous class in a graphic organizer. He wanted to learn not just what his students got from yesterday's lesson, but how they understood it. Their mind map also showed relationships between items and hierarchies. Students turned this in within ten minutes. While students were completing these, Victor wrote on the board the new daily graphic organizer, with missing pieces on it. (The gaps create curiosity.) Once the students completed their written retrieval work, they turned it in.

Students were then asked to copy the new graphic organizer on their paper. Victor collected them and sorted them quickly to identify any gaps in student learning from the day before. Both the teacher and the students completed their new task in the same amount of time. The students received their papers and saw how they did. To score them, Victor used a number from 1–5 (1 is low, and 5 is high). The teacher asked students with low scores to rework their summary up front. His relationship with the class was strong, and there was no blaming or snickering. The learning culture of the class was "We all make mistakes, so let's all learn from them." Every student was treated with dignity, so no student was embarrassed to rework his or her assignment. It was important for the teacher to fix any mistakes from yesterday before moving ahead into new material. In mathematics, every day is critical. Victor coached them along to ensure accuracy. This gave the students and Victor feedback on how well (or poorly) he taught yesterday.

Then, he introduced new material to the whole class. Using the schematic shown up front, he condensed new class knowledge, and then detailed, again condensed, and again detailed in content pulses. The teacher (and students) used color coding on the notes, with arrows and drawings to show different values and properties of the content. He always supported and never criticized students.

Victor's class was always about understanding and memory. Students used the notes to cue their memories. He based grades on the aggregate of many weekly quizzes. His primary goal was to provide his students with the confidence and skills to succeed. With confidence, students kept trying until they got it. Homework was 100 percent optional. He gave his students 100 to 150 problems at the outset of the semester, and they could do any of them at any time. Most did all of them. To me, some of this teacher's strengths are:

- Structured and guided instruction (using schema, worked examples, and so on)
- Big-to-small picture (condensed and detailed)
- Sky-high expectations (100 percent success plus homework)
- Relationships (He is each student's greatest ally.)
- Feedback (given to his students and to him, the teacher)

- Low threat (low stress; never any embarrassment for students)
- Choice (on homework and how students illustrate the learning)

Notice that he didn't do everything in this book. But he was very good at the key things: high expectations, feedback, engagement, support, relationships, control, and low threat plus big picture and detailed schemas. Now, I have a question for you. If someone gave you the classroom-proven model for highly successful teaching, would you use it?

Action Steps

Many teachers do not do consistent lesson planning. The lesson plan has to include not just what you are teaching, but what the students should be doing and how you are teaching it. Most make the mistake of not putting the student achievement and mindset boosters in the lesson plan to ramp up results. Finally, most plan them collaboratively. You can be different.

Figure A.2 provides a checklist with the mindsets' strategies throughout the book. Use this refresher list to make some decisions. Which of these items will be your starter steps?

Student Mindsets

Check the boxes where you can upgrade your students' brains.

Positivity Mindset
- ☐ Boost optimism and hope.
- ☐ Build positive attitudes.
- ☐ Foster choice, control, and relevancy.
- ☐ Change the emotional set point.

Enrichment Mindset
- ☐ Manage the cognitive load.
- ☐ Develop better thinking skills.
- ☐ Enhance study skills and vocabulary.
- ☐ Build better memory.

Graduation Mindset
- ☐ Support alternative solutions.
- ☐ Prepare for college and careers.

Figure A.2: Checklist for changing mindsets.

continued on next page ⇨

Getting Started With Students

- The specific strategies I will begin to use are: _____
- I'll start doing this beginning: _____
- I will assess progress for my feedback on: _____
- I plan to have this strategy completely automated by: _____

Personal Strategies

Check the boxes where you can upgrade your own brain.

- ☐ **The positivity mindset:** I am an optimistic and grateful ally who helps students build a successful narrative of their future.
- ☐ **The enrichment mindset:** I know brains can change. I can grow and change myself first. Then, I can build powerful cognitive skills in my students.
- ☐ **The graduation mindset:** Focus on what matters. Be an ally to help students graduate college and career ready.

Getting Started

- The specific mindset I will begin to use is: _____
- I'll start doing this beginning: _____
- I will assess progress for my feedback on: _____
- I plan to have this strategy completely automated by: _____

Visit go.SolutionTree.com/instruction for a reproducible version of this figure.

Quick Consolidation

This chapter focuses on rich lesson planning. You may know the general steps (check data, turn data into meaning, discuss concerns, break down the meaning into actionable work, make learning goals, turn the work into lesson plans, use quality feedback standards for all, establish implementation goals, use frequent feedback from coaches or school leaders, get feedback on instruction from colleagues or leaders watching your lesson, and never stop improving). However, the real value in this chapter is that powerful lesson plans include the process (collaboration, preassessment, relevance and buy-in, and attribution). By integrating what is really important in lesson planning, you can start getting the richer teaching that I have invited you to enjoy. Teaching low-income students well is hard work. The beauty of this process is that you now have, in your hands, some powerful tools to make the magic happen. Are you going to be the teacher students get changes their life? We all need you to be the richer teacher this year. Can we all count on you?

Appendix B
Running Your Own Brain

Like most teachers, you don't think about your brain every day because it is so *you* that it is hard to stand back and reflect about something that is, well, embedded in you. Yet, it absolutely runs the show. Everything in your life is run by your brain. Earlier in the book, you were introduced to the positivity mindset, the enrichment mindset, and, then, the graduation mindset. Now, I'm going to give you the toolbox to use all the mindset tools effectively. It focuses on who you think you are and what you can do about it. It is the Running Your Own Brain toolbox.

Learning to Run Your Own Brain

Your brain can change in an instant. If it is a bad change, it could come from drug abuse, a car accident, an addiction, or a traumatic event. Chronic stress brings impaired social skills, working memory, decision making, and diminished interest in fun things (Bogdan & Pizzagalli, 2006). Your brain activates both the sympathetic and parasympathetic nervous system, so you feel stress everywhere in your body. Stress is a physiological response to a perception of a lack of control over an aversive situation or person.

Your brain changes all day long, every day, as you input and record information, experience emotions, and store memories. These changes are small but cumulative. New memories gradually change your life story. To help students from poverty succeed, it's good to know how to run your own brain. I want you not just to survive but thrive in a crazy, tough workplace. You'll want to make the changes happen systematically and purposefully. Random changes rarely make miracles happen. This book is not a one-size-fits-all guide; I focus on just one objective: helping you become sensational at your job.

I can show you how to navigate the process of running your own brain. Your brain processes countless inputs every day. Individual brain structures (like the cerebellum) do, of course, play a part in how your brain works. However, it is more accurate to talk of systems, which are aggregates of theme-connected parts. I have invested a lot of time trying to figure out how my own brain works best and how to work with it, not against it. I've talked to neuroscientists and attended conferences, and I'm also a member of the invitation-only Society for Neuroscience with over thirty thousand members.

For the sake of brevity and potency, I will discuss just three systems. Each system has multiple, ongoing, powerful effects on your success as a teacher in a high-poverty school. They are actually designed by nature, and the way you live your life either pushes them one way (to thrive) or another way (toward struggle). The truth is, you can run these brain systems your way if you are purposeful about it. It's your choice. These three brain systems are the critical neurobiological linchpins for high-performance teaching of students from low socioeconomic backgrounds. Great teachers likely have all three working in their favor.

1. **The meaning-making narrative system (frontal lobes and left temporal lobe):** This system creates ongoing stories in your brain. It helps develop part of your personality and character through your stories.

2. **The stress-response system (hypothalamus, adrenals, and prefrontal cortex):** This system is about your grit and persistence. What stress do you tolerate, how do you cope, and how well do you persist and function under stress?

3. **The reward system (nucleus accumbens, ventral tegmental area, and prefrontal cortex):** The reward system activates good feelings for you at work (or not). What is important to you? This system helps you stay focused on the daily and long-term events that make your brain happy.

Let's learn how to activate each of these so that the changes you want to make after reading this book become more automatic and lasting. Your brain should value your work in ways that bring you joy (spontaneous pleasure as well as long-term satisfaction—*eudaimonic* pleasure; see page 55).

Your Brain's Meaning-Making Narrative System

The meaning-making narrative system ensures you are a story-maker. Your brain seeks the reasons for why and how something happens (Gazzaniga, 1998). Bert Cohler (1980), a pioneer in psychology, shows that our stories and narratives guide our lives. This system comprises the activity in your verbal language hemisphere (usually the left side) and the seamless activation of memories that support the narrative (your temporal lobes). When something bad happens, and someone says, "That must have happened for a reason," it's *almost* true; it's just backward. The reason didn't come first; the event came first. Then, we humans try to make sense of a world that is often random, chaotic, and certainly unfair. Meaning making is natural in people of all ages (Hammack & Toolis, 2014). To maintain some sanity when things seem disconnected or unsettling, we create alternative explanations. We often stitch together a series of unrelated events, surprise circumstances, and unusually good or bad events. Our brains need an everyday narrative about life; it is part of what helps us survive and thrive.

Your left hemisphere helps you create these stories about your life and others' lives. In fact, every culture is built on the stories that the leaders tell and sell to others. See figure B.1 for a visual of this system.

The Meaning-Making Narrative System

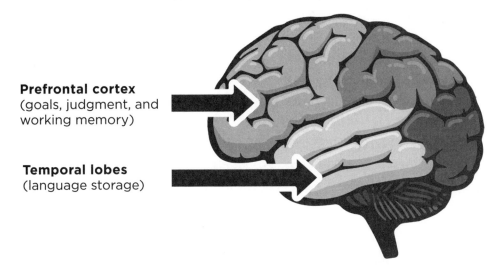

Prefrontal cortex
(goals, judgment, and working memory)

Temporal lobes
(language storage)

Figure B.1: Your brain's narrative system.

Everyone needs some kind of a narrative to move forward in life. Your brain's storytelling function is the basis for all novels, campfire stories, pop songs, movie plots, amateur and research-oriented explanations, and even political campaigns. It is the way we process, understand, and remember the experiences of life. It is our mechanism, in many ways, for a personal form of sanity.

Teacher Implications

So, how does meaning making play out in your quest to become a more awesome teacher? Teacher narratives begin early in life. The experiences you had as an elementary student shape your teaching and what you do at work. As you go through the process to become a teacher, your classmates influence the narrative in your head about what to expect. Once you start teaching, your colleagues, books, conferences, district personnel, and school leadership all contribute new narratives about teaching. Over time, you amass a series of stories about how things should be, how things are, and how things will be in the future.

This is why, in each chapter, I remind you that your narratives influence your decision making. For example, what if you were considering switching to another school and the buzz around your campus was that your favorite administrator was leaving? What if an unpopular candidate were likely to replace him or her? An uncertain future threatens the current narrative about who will stay at the school (good times in the past). As a result of this new narrative, you might give less effort. Alternatively, you might follow your favorite administrator to a new school and hope the new school is better. The narrative is already influencing your behaviors—for better or worse.

You can't control everything, but you *can* control your response to nearly everything. The narrative system asks, "What is causing what?" and asks you, "Whose fault is it? What are you going to do? " Manage the story in your head more proactively (after all, it's *you* making up the story), and you'll manage your life.

It is counterproductive to allow other narratives that are negative, hurtful, and toxic to become your narrative; life is short. Add those narratives to your life, and soon things go downhill, unless, of course, you can manage your life by learning to run your own brain. Here's how you can do it.

Action Steps

The world is simply full of narratives. You can create fresh life stories about your decision making. If you can take on the new narratives, consider the following two action steps.

1. Take on one new mindset each month. Write it down. Type it out. Print copies to post at home (next to your bathroom mirror) and in your classroom.

2. Ensure you read the new mindset twice a day. Once you read it, affirm it. Say, "Now that's me. That's what I'm talking about."

Now, let's work on your stress.

Your Brain's Stress-Response System

This system stretches across multiple brain and body areas. Areas include the hypothalamus, the pituitary gland, the cerebral cortex, the heart, and the adrenals. In addition, specific stress states activate memories in visual, temporal (for sounds), or amygdalar (for feelings) areas. In other words, much of your brain feels threatened when you feel stressed. That's why it can influence you so much. See figure B.2 for a visual of the stress-response system.

Teacher Implications

Teacher stress impacts moodiness and job satisfaction (Serrano, Moya-Albiol, & Salvador, 2014). When you are relaxed and teach well, your body and brain are proactive, and you make better decisions. When you feel stressed, you're being exposed to uncontrollable situations or people. You become reactive and less thoughtful. Life changes can be stressful. Staff can be stressful. Students can be stressful. Traffic and bills can be stressful. Accountability with minimal time to plan and learn can be stressful.

The Stress-Response System

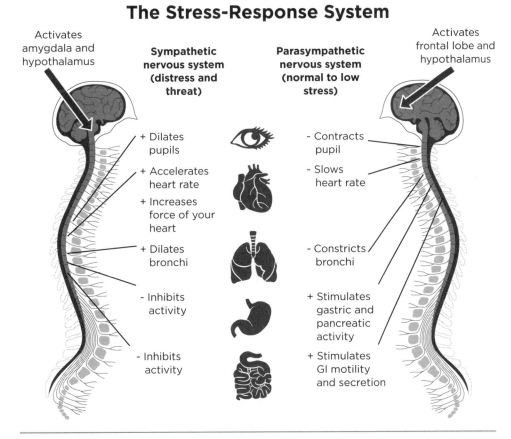

Activates amygdala and hypothalamus	**Sympathetic nervous system (distress and threat)**	**Parasympathetic nervous system (normal to low stress)**	**Activates frontal lobe and hypothalamus**

+ Dilates pupils

+ Accelerates heart rate

+ Increases force of your heart

+ Dilates bronchi

- Inhibits activity

- Inhibits activity

- Contracts pupil

- Slows heart rate

- Constricts bronchi

+ Stimulates gastric and pancreatic activity

+ Stimulates GI motility and secretion

Figure B.2: Your brain's stress-response system.

What you need is a renewed understanding (the truth) about stress, so here it is: there is no stress out there in the world. It's all in your head. That's right; on a weekend, there is no stress in your classroom (or on the campus). There is no stress at school, no stress from your staff, and no stress from your students. No one else stresses you out. Your brain, that you run, stresses you out.

Why would your brain stress you out all the time? In evolutionary terms, stressors were connected to survival. They included enemies, food scarcity, shelter, animals, water, safety, and health. Those factors remain to varying degrees, but new ones have joined them. We get stressed over who just got hired, new standards, someone cutting in line, what our children post online, and a missing bank statement. We get stressed when students are tardy or when they mouth off or disengage in class. Add these daily stressors to hundreds of others, and you get a very stressed body. That's bad—unless you can manage your life by learning to run your own brain. Until you do, you'll never become awesome at teaching students from poverty, as your margin of error is thinner and your students' stressors will exacerbate your own. What you tolerate, how you cope, and your grit are critical features of your future teaching success (Farr, 2010).

Your brain makes a decision about whether to develop stress based on only two factors: relevance and control. First, when the brain notices an environmental (or internalized) averse prompt, it asks, "Is this relevant to me?" If it is not, you will experience little or no stress. Second, if it is relevant, your brain asks, "Do I have any control or agency to influence the outcome of this situation?" If you have little or no control, you get stressed. If you have a good deal of control, you get energized to take action. Stress is that simple (and that complex). To minimize stress, you'll need to minimize relevant factors over which you have no control. See figure B.3 for a visual.

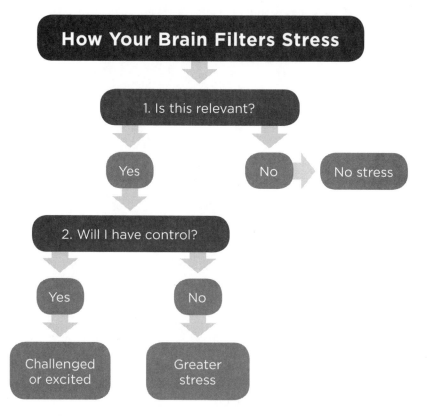

Figure B.3: Stress filters.

What predicts success when teaching high-poverty students is a narrative of perseverance, stress regulation, and grit—having a strong, go-forward attitude (Duckworth, Quinn, & Seligman, 2009). Do you have those traits? If not, you can teach them to yourself. After all, you're going to teach them to your students.

Researchers have made very little progress in linking teacher effectiveness and retention to commonly known interview factors at the time of hire (Robertson-Kraft & Duckworth, 2014). The tough rigors of teaching at Title I schools suggest the possibility of specific qualities for thriving. In a study examining the predictive validity of grit in 457 teachers at low-income schools, teachers who scored higher in grit outperformed their less hardy colleagues and were less likely to leave the school (Robertson-Kraft & Duckworth, 2014). These tenacious teachers were simply more likely to stay and succeed.

If you think being a highflier, a teacher in the top 25 percent academically in Title I schools, is way too much work, keep reading. A study surveyed twelve high-poverty schools on every imaginable topic, including hours worked per day at work, at home, and on weekends. Half of the high-poverty schools were low performing and half were high performing. The over-worked staff were the low-performing teachers, although they worked more hours per week than the high performers (Jensen, 2014). The key isn't to work more hours; it is to work the same or fewer but be more thoughtful and make changes quickly when things are not working. It will save your soul and help your students succeed.

Action Steps

Here are the optimal ways to reduce stress. First, start with this affirmation every day: "There is no stress out there; I can manage my own stress to become healthier and happier." Second, stop the DATS (daily annoying triggered self-talk) that brings you down. For example, don't say things to yourself like, "I don't think she likes me. Maybe I shouldn't sit with her." Change that internal dialogue to something neutral: "I'm unsure of her. I think today, I'll move along and enjoy the day." Third, do what makes you happy and helps you feel in control; feed your soul. Consider the following activities: twelve-minute daily workouts, seven hours of sleep every night, ten minutes of stretching or yoga every day, brief talks or journal entries about your day, weekly gratitude sharing, and hobbies. Fourth, develop coping tools, and use the mind-over-matter strategy: "Will this stressor even matter a week from now?" Because if it won't matter a week from now, you might reconsider the frustration and energy you're expending now. Figure B.4 offers some strategies to rewire your brain's stress-response system.

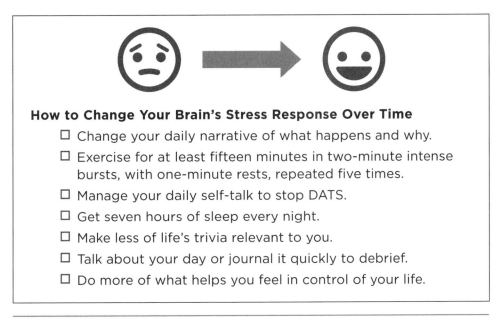

How to Change Your Brain's Stress Response Over Time

☐ Change your daily narrative of what happens and why.

☐ Exercise for at least fifteen minutes in two-minute intense bursts, with one-minute rests, repeated five times.

☐ Manage your daily self-talk to stop DATS.

☐ Get seven hours of sleep every night.

☐ Make less of life's trivia relevant to you.

☐ Talk about your day or journal it quickly to debrief.

☐ Do more of what helps you feel in control of your life.

Figure B.4: Stress-response system checklist.

*Visit **go.SolutionTree.com/instruction** for a reproducible version of this figure.*

Pick one to add to your rotating list of options or write it down for later. Remember, take action to get control and redirect your attention to another, less stressful task (McEwen, 2002). In short, as you master your stress-response system, you'll generate more joy, peace of mind, and energy. Now you have the attitude and the strategy to release yourself from debilitating stressors.

Your Brain's Reward System

Rewards (or the anticipation of them) make you feel good. The type of reward varies from the unexpected surprise to a predicted good thing that was actually great, not marginal. Often, physical gifts can be a reward, but your brain is as likely to feel rewarded by a five-dollar ice cream cone as it is for a five-hundred-dollar ice cream maker. Rewards are typically about feeling good in the short term, but they run our lives (Fredrickson & Losada, 2005). Figure B.5 is an outline of your pathway to rewarding behavior.

Your Brain's Reward System

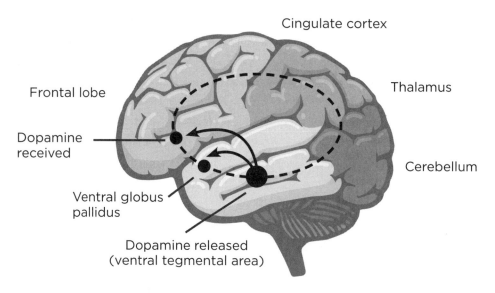

Figure B.5: Your brain's reward system.

When you anticipate something good, your brain generates dopamine, the neurotransmitter of reward. Note the path starts at the center and bottom of your brain. Dopamine also helps you feel good with unexpected rewards. Knowing that this process is on your side (most of the time) is reassuring. Abuse of this system, though, can result in addiction. For example, I love the aroma of fresh coffee in the can or bag, and even brewed coffee, but I am not a coffee drinker. However, I do like a morning drink.

Decades ago, after my first trip to Hawaii, I was hooked on drinking pineapple juice in the morning. I felt like I *had* to have it. Then, over time, I switched over to orange juice.

Soon, I felt like I *had* to have it. Then, I switched over to energy drinks (mostly caffeine and sugar). I felt like I *had* to have them each morning. Then, my wife suggested that they are not as healthy as coffee (which she drinks). So, I switched over to coconut juice. I now feel like I *have* to have it each morning. The pattern is pretty clear; our brains can get hooked on almost anything, good or bad. Just be careful of what you're hooked on, and consider the take-home reward and your health.

Teacher Implications

In school, this feel-good system drives many of your daily joys. Every student who struggles brings you another opportunity for a reward, because that student succeeds largely because of you. When you care about student achievement, every strategy you use that works triggers a reward for your brain. So does every song you play in class that works. Every time you help students raise their class scores, your brain gets a reward. The bottom line is this: the more invested you get in students' success, the greater the rewards for you (as well as for them). This is why you'll want to develop the positivity mindset; doing it for your students also benefits you too. Make it happen with fresh class routines, academic optimism, and a positive class culture.

Action Steps

You'll need to take seriously the notion of noticing, creating, and accentuating the positives. This will not happen without your focus and intention. What policies, practices, and procedures are in place to help yourself and others notice and appreciate every single sign of progress in your class? Unless you set up multiple systems for feedback and acknowledgment, your class will have little or no positive energy and will become a chore to teach.

- When you ask students to raise their hands to contribute, do you thank them 100 percent of the time with eye contact and a smile?

- Do you establish a positive class climate daily? For example, when students finish a quiz, do you ask them to turn to their neighbors and say, "I'm flying to graduation!" when they receive a 70 percent or higher?

- When students arrive early or on time, do you notice it and thank them? When students help others, do you mention it and thank them?

In short, never let a chance to notice the good go to waste. You want to use every opportunity you can to make your class awesome and help your students on the path to graduation.

With these three systems in mind, you can run your own brain.

Final Consolidation

This whole book presents one major theme: no excuses. High-performing schools progress without making any excuses; we see students working hard and knowing they will succeed because the staff won't let them fail. Three mindsets are introduced, and any of them can move you forward. On a final note, you might have noticed that this book is not just quick teacher strategies. It is more than that. You are at a career crossroads. You now know you can change, adapt, and grow, or you can wish and hope that you'll get a better batch of students next year.

If you have struggled to have high-performing students in the past, this resource can help you get there. Why do I say that? I study high performers for a living and share their mindsets and tools. I am inviting you to allow this book's process of learning, growing, and applying what you learn to change you. In turn, the changes you make will change the students you teach, so that they succeed.

We all know that your students may be difficult, frustrating, and thoroughly a pain at times. But there is a lesson you can take from them. Every student you have has the capacity to unleash an extraordinary passion from within. If you want your students to succeed, you must connect with them as individuals. Only then can you set loose the tidal wave of continual effort. The way you will become highly effective in your job is by learning how to connect deeply in ways the students can feel and hear every day.

When you do embrace the mindsets and action steps in this book, and when you do unleash your new narratives, mindsets, and strategies, you can expect a richer life beyond anything you've ever dreamed of. That's a promise. I know; I have done it. Now, I am hoping you'll be looking forward to every opportunity to help students succeed. Unfortunately, not enough teachers have been doing that. But I think you are different. Are you? Will you become a champion for students?

References and Resources

Aas, M., Henry, C., Andreassen, O. A., Bellivier, F., Melle, I., & Etain, B. (2016). The role of childhood trauma in bipolar disorders. *International Journal of Bipolar Disorders*, *4*(1), 2.

Adler, A. D., Conklin, L. R., & Strunk, D. R. (2013). Quality of coping skills predicts depressive symptom reactivity over repeated stressors. *Journal of Clinical Psychology*, *69*, 1228–1238.

Aikens, N. L., & Barbarin, O. (2008). Socioeconomic differences in reading trajectories: The contribution of family, neighborhood, and school contexts. *Journal of Educational Psychology*, *100*(2), 235–251.

Algina, J., & Olejnik, S. (2003). Conducting power analyses for ANOVA and ANCOVA in between-subjects designs. *Evaluation and the Health Professions*, *26*(3), 288–314.

Algoe, S. B. (2012) Find, remind, and bind: The functions of gratitude in everyday relationships. *Social and Personality Psychology Compass*, *6*, 455–469.

Algoe, S. B., & Fredrickson, B. L. (2011). Emotional fitness and the movement of affective science from lab to field. *American Psychologist*, *66*(1), 35–42.

Algoe, S. B., Haidt, J., & Gable, S. L. (2008). Beyond reciprocity: Gratitude and relationships in everyday life. *Emotion*, *8*(3), 425–429.

Alloway, T. P., & Alloway, R. G. (2010). Investigating the predictive roles of working memory and IQ in academic attainment. *Journal of Experimental Child Psychology*, *106*(1), 20–29.

Amat, J., Paul, E., Zarza, C., Watkins, L. R., & Maier, S. F. (2006). Previous experience with behavioral control over stress blocks the behavioral and dorsal raphe nucleus activating effects of later uncontrollable stress: Role of the ventral medial prefrontal cortex. *Journal of Neuroscience*, *26*(51), 13264–13272.

Amy Purdy. (n.d.). In *Wikipedia*. Accessed at https://en.wikipedia.org/wiki/Amy_Purdy on May 14, 2016.

Asbury, C., & Rich, B. (Eds.). (2008). *Learning, arts, and the brain: The Dana Consortium report on arts and cognition*. New York: The Dana Foundation. Accessed at www.dana .org/uploadedFiles/News_and_Publications/Special_Publications/Learning,%20Arts%20 and%20the%20Brain_ArtsAndCognition_Compl.pdf on January 6, 2016.

Au, J., Sheehan, E., Tsai, N., Duncan, G. J., Buschkuehl, M., & Jaeggi, S. M. (2015). Improving fluid intelligence with training on working memory: A meta-analysis. *Psychonomic Bulletin and Review*, *22*(2), 366–377.

Bailey, T. C., Eng, W., Frisch, M. B., & Snyder, C. R. (2007). Hope and optimism as related to life satisfaction. *Journal of Positive Psychology*, *2*(3), 168–175.

Bankrate. (2012). *Financial Security Index down slightly*. Accessed at www.bankrate.com /finance/consumer-index/financial-security-charts-1112.aspx on January 6, 2016.

Baratta, M. V., Zarza, C. M., Gomez, D. M., Campeau, S., Watkins, L. R., & Maier, S. F. (2009). Selective activation of dorsal raphe nucleus-projecting neurons in the ventral medial prefrontal cortex by controllable stress. *European Journal of Neuroscience*, *30*(6), 1111–1116.

Barbarin, O., Iruka, I. U., Harradine, C., Winn, D. M., McKinney, M. K., & Taylor, L. C. (2013). Development of social-emotional competence in boys of color: A cross-sectional cohort analysis from pre-K to second grade. *American Journal of Orthopsychiatry*, *83*(2), 145–155.

Barnett, S. M., & Ceci, S. J. (2002). When and where do we apply what we learn?: A taxonomy for far transfer. *Psychological Bulletin*, *128*(4), 612–637.

Behnke, A. O., Piercy, K. W., & Diversi, M. (2004). Educational and occupational aspirations of Latino youth and their parents. *Hispanic Journal of Behavioral Sciences*, *26*(1), 16–35.

Beierholm, U., Guitart-Masip, M., Economides, M., Chowdhury, R., Düzel, E., Dolan, R., et al. (2013). Dopamine modulates reward-related vigor. *Neuropsychopharmacology*, *38*(8), 1495–1503.

Berger, M., & Sarnyai, Z. (2015). "More than skin deep": Stress neurobiology and mental health consequences of racial discrimination. *Stress*, *18*(1), 1–10.

Berger, J., Heinrichs, M., von Dawans, B., Way, B. M., & Chen, F. S. (2016). Cortisol modulates men's affiliative responses to acute social stress. *Psychoneuroendocrinology*, *63*, 1–9.

Berghorst, L. H., Bogdan, R., Frank, M. J., & Pizzagalli, D. A. (2013). Acute stress selectively reduces reward sensitivity. *Frontiers in Human Neuroscience*, *7*(133), 1–15.

Berns, G. S., Blaine, K., Prietula, M. J., & Pye, B. E. (2013). Short- and long-term effects of a novel on connectivity in the brain. *Brain Connectivity*, *3*(6), 590–600.

Best, J. R. (2010). Effects of physical activity on children's executive function: Contributions of experimental research on aerobic exercise. *Developmental Review*, *30*(4), 331–351.

Bezold, C. P., Konty, K. J., Day, S. E., Berger, M., Harr, L., Larkin, M., et al. (2014). The effects of changes in physical fitness on academic performance among New York City youth. *Journal of Adolescent Health*, *55*(6), 774–781.

Biemiller, A. (2003). Vocabulary needed if children are to read well. *Reading Psychology*, *24*, 323–335.

Biggs, J. (1987). *Student approaches to learning and studying Hawthorn*. Camberwell, Victoria, Australia: Australian Council for Educational Research.

Blackwell, L. S., Trzesniewski, K. H., & Dweck, C. S. (2007). Implicit theories of intelligence predict achievement across an adolescent transition: A longitudinal study and an intervention. *Child Development, 78*(1), 246–263.

Blake, D. T., Heiser, M. A., Caywood, M., & Merzenich, M. M. (2006). Experience-dependent adult cortical plasticity requires cognitive association between sensation and reward. *Neuron, 52*(2), 371–381.

Blokland, G. A. M., McMahon, K. L., Thompson, P. M., Martin, N. G., de Zubicaray, G. I., & Wright, M. J. (2011). Heritability of working memory brain activation. *Journal of Neuroscience, 31*(30), 10882–10890.

Bogdan, R., & Pizzagalli, D. A. (2006). Acute stress reduces reward responsiveness: Implications for depression. *Biological Psychiatry, 60*(10), 1147–1154.

Bolte, A., Goschkey, T., & Kuhl, J. (2003). Emotion and intuition: Effects of positive and negative mood on implicit judgments of semantic coherence. *Psychological Science, 14*(5), 416–421.

Brown, B. (2012). *Daring greatly: How the courage to be vulnerable transforms the way we live, love, parent, and lead.* New York: Gotham Books.

Brown, B. (2015). *Rising strong.* New York: Spiegel & Grau.

Brown, J., Cooper-Kuhn, C. M., Kempermann, G., van Praag, H., Winkler, J., Gage, F. H., et al. (2003). Enriched environment and physical activity stimulate hippocampal but not olfactory bulb neurogenesis. *European Journal of Neuroscience, 17*(10), 2042–2046.

Bruininks, P., & Malle, B. F. (2005). Distinguishing hope from optimism and related affective states. *Motivation and Emotion, 29*(4), 324–352.

Budde, H., Voelcker-Rehage, C., Pietrabyk-Kendziorra, S., Ribeiro, P., & Tidow, G. (2008). Acute coordinative exercise improves attentional performance in adolescents. *Neuroscience Letters, 441*(2), 219–223.

Bui, Q. (2015, February 5). Map: The most common* job in every state. *Planet Money: The Economy Explained.* Accessed at www.npr.org/sections/money/2015/02/05/382664837/map-the-most-common-job-in-every-state on January 6, 2016.

Bull, R., Espy, K. A., & Wiebe, S. A. (2008). Short-term memory, working memory, and executive functioning in preschoolers: Longitudinal predictors of mathematical achievement at age 7 years. *Developmental Neuropsychology, 33*(3), 205–228.

Butler-Barnes, S. T., Williams, T. T., & Chavous, T. M. (2012). Racial pride and religiosity among African American boys: Implications for academic motivation and achievement. *Journal of Youth and Adolescence, 41*(4), 486–498.

Caeyenberghs, K., Leemans, A., Heitger, M. H., Leunissen, I., Dhollander, T., Sunaert, S., et al. (2012). Graph analysis of functional brain networks for cognitive control of action in traumatic brain injury. *Brain, 135*(4), 1293–1307.

Canfield, J. (2015). *The success principles: How to get from where you are to where you want to be* (10th anniv. ed.). New York: William Morrow.

Canfield, J., & Hansen, M. V. (2013). *Chicken soup for the soul* (20th anniv. ed.). Cos Cob, CT: Chicken Soup for the Soul.

Carlson, S. A., Fulton, J. E., Lee, S. M., Maynard, L. M., Brown, D. R., Kohl, H. W., III., et al. (2008). Physical education and academic achievement in elementary school: Data from the early childhood longitudinal study. *American Journal of Public Health, 98*(4), 721–727.

Carter, S. C. (2001). *No excuses: Lessons from 21 high-performing, high-poverty schools.* Washington, DC: Heritage Foundation.

Catalino, L. I., & Fredrickson, B. L. (2011). A Tuesday in the life of a flourisher: The role of positive emotional reactivity in optimal mental health. *Emotion, 11*(4), 938–950.

Catalino, L. I., Algoe, S. B., & Fredrickson, B. L. (2014). Prioritizing positivity: an effective approach to pursuing happiness? *Emotion, 14,* 1155–1161.

Catterall, J. S., Chapleau, R., & Iwanaga, J. (1999). Involvement in the arts and human development: General involvement and intensive involvement in music and theater arts. In E. Fiske (Ed.), *Champions of change: The impact of the arts on learning* (pp. 1–18). Washington, DC: Arts Education Partnership.

Catterall, J. S. (2003). Research and assessment on the arts and learning: Education policy implications of recent research on the arts and academic and social development. *Journal for Learning Through Music, 3*(2003), 103–109.

Catterall, J. S. (2009). *Doing well and doing good by doing art: The effects of education in the visual and performing arts on the achievements and values of young adults.* Los Angeles: Imagination Group.

Catterall, J. S., Dumais, S. A., & Hampden-Thompson, G. (2012). *The arts and achievement in at-risk youth: Findings from four longitudinal studies* (Research Report No. 55). Washington, DC: National Endowment for the Arts.

Ceci, S. J., & Williams, W. M. (1997). Schooling, intelligence, and income. *American Psychologist, 52*(10), 1051–1058.

Center for Public Education. (2005). *High-performing, high-poverty schools: Research review.* Accessed at www.centerforpubliceducation.org/Main-Menu/Organizing-a-school/High-performing-high-poverty-schools-At-a-glance-/High-performing-high-poverty-schools-Research-review.html on May 18, 2016.

Cepeda, N. J., Coburn, N., Rohrer, D., Wixted, J. T., Mozer, M. C., & Pashler, H. (2009). Optimizing distributed practice: Theoretical analysis and practical implications. *Experimental Psychology, 56*(4), 236–246.

Chan, C. S., Rhodes, J. E., Howard, W. J., Lowe, S. R., Schwartz, S. E. O., & Herrera, C. (2013). Pathways of influence in school-based mentoring: The mediating role of parent and teacher relationships. *Journal of School Psychology, 51*(1), 129–142.

Clamp, M., Fry, B., Kamal, M., Xie, X., Cuff, J., Lin, M. F., et al. (2007). Distinguishing protein-coding and noncoding genes in the human genome. *Proceedings of the National Academy of Sciences of the United States of America, 104*(49), 19428–19433.

Coe, D. P., Peterson, T., Blair, C., Schutten, M. C., & Peddie, H. (2013). Physical fitness, academic achievement, and socioeconomic status in school-aged youth. *Journal of School Health, 83*(7), 500–507.

Cohler, B. J. (1980). Personal narrative and life course. In P. Baltes & O. G. Brim Jr. (Eds.), *Life span development and behavior* (Vol. 4, pp. 205–241). New York: Academic Press.

Cohn, M. A., & Fredrickson, B. L. (2010). In search of durable positive psychology interventions: Predictors and consequences of long-term positive behavior change. *Journal of Positive Psychology, 5*(5), 355–366.

Cohn, M. A., Fredrickson, B. L., Brown, S. L., Mikels, J. A., & Conway, A. M. (2009). Happiness unpacked: Positive emotions increase life satisfaction by building resilience. *Emotion, 9*(3), 361–368.

Conway, A. R., Kane, M. J., & Engle, R. W. (2003). Working memory capacity and its relation to general intelligence. *Trends in Cognitive Sciences, 7*(12), 547–552.

Cook, S. W., Mitchell, Z., & Goldin-Meadow, S. (2008). Gesturing makes learning last. *Cognition, 106*(2), 1047–1058.

Cowan, N. (2010). The magical mystery four: How is working memory capacity limited, and why? *Current Directions in Psychological Science, 19*(1), 51–57.

Crocker, R. (2015). Emotional testimonies: An ethnographic study of emotional suffering related to migration from Mexico to Arizona. *Frontiers in Public Health, 3*(177).

Crone, E. A., Wendelken, C., Donohue, S., van Leijenhorst, L., & Bunge, S. A. (2006). Neurocognitive development of the ability to manipulate information in working memory. *Proceedings of the National Academy of Sciences of the United States of America, 103*(24), 9315–9320.

Davis, O. S., Butcher, L. M., Docherty, S. J., Meaburn, E. L., Curtis, C. J. C., Simpson, M. A., et al. (2010). A three-stage genome-wide association study of general cognitive ability: Hunting the small effects. *Behavior Genetics, 40*(6), 759–767.

de Bono, E. (1999). *Six thinking hats* (Rev. and updated ed.). Boston: Back Bay.

Delgado, M. R., Nearing, K. I., LeDoux, J. E., & Phelps, E. A. (2008). Neural circuitry underlying the regulation of conditioned fear and its relation to extinction. *Neuron, 59*(5), 829–838.

De Smedt, B., Janssen, R., Bouwens, K., Verschaffel, L., Boets, B., & Ghesquière, P. (2009). Working memory and individual differences in mathematics achievement: A longitudinal study from first grade to second grade. *Journal of Experimental Child Psychology, 103*(2), 186–201.

Disabato, D. J., Goodman, F. R., Kashdan, T. B., Short, J. L., & Jarden, A. (2015). Different types of well-being?: A cross-cultural examination of hedonic and eudaimonic well-being. *Psychological Assessment, 28*, 471–482.

Dolcos S., Hu, Y., Iordan, A. D., Moore, M., & Dolcos, F. (2016). Optimism and the brain: trait optimism mediates the protective role of the orbitofrontal cortex gray matter volume against anxiety. *Social Cognitive and Affective Neuroscience, 11*, 263–271.

Dubois, L., Ohm Kyvik, K., Girard, M., Tatone-Tokuda, F., Pérusse, D., Hjelmborg, J., et al. (2012). Genetic and environmental contributions to weight, height, and BMI from birth to 19 years of age: An international study of over 12,000 twin pairs. *PLOS ONE, 7*(2).

Duckworth, A. L., Kirby, T. A., Gollwitzer, A., & Oettingen, G. (2013). From fantasy to action: Mental contrasting with implementation intentions (MCII) improves academic performance in children. *Social Psychological and Personality Science, 4*(6), 745–753.

Duckworth, A. L., Quinn, P. D., & Seligman, M. E. P. (2009). Positive predictors of teacher effectiveness. *Journal of Positive Psychology, 4*(6), 540–547.

Duyme, M., Dumaret, A.-C., & Tomkiewicz, S. (1999). How can we boost IQs of "dull children"?: A late adoption study. *Proceedings of the National Academy of Sciences of the United States of America, 96*(15), 8790–8794.

Dweck, C. S. (1999). *Self-theories: Their role in motivation, personality, and development.* Philadelphia: Psychology Press.

Dweck, C. S. (2008). *Mindset: The new psychology of success—How we can learn to fulfill our potential.* New York: Ballantine.

Economic Policy Institute. (2014). *Real median household income, all households and working-age, 1979–2013 (2013 dollars).* Accessed at www.stateofworkingamerica.org /charts/real-median-household-income on January 6, 2016.

Emmons, R. A. (2007). *Thanks!: How the new science of gratitude can make you happier.* Boston: Houghton Mifflin.

Emmons, R. A., & Stern, R. (2013). Gratitude as a psychotherapeutic intervention. *Journal of Clinical Psychology, 69,* 846–855.

Engineer, N. D., Engineer, C. T., Reed, A. C., Pandya, P. K., Jakkamsetti, V., Moucha, R., et al. (2012). Inverted-U function relating cortical plasticity and task difficulty. *Neuroscience, 205,* 81–90.

Engle, R. W. (2001). What is working memory capacity? In H. L. Roediger III, J. S. Nairne, I. Neath, & A. M. Suprenant (Eds.), *The nature of remembering: Essays in honor of Robert G. Crowder* (pp. 297–314). Washington, DC: American Psychological Association.

Epel, E. S., Blackburn, E. H., Lin, J., Dhabhar, F. S., Adler, N. E., Morrow, J. D., et al. (2004). Accelerated telomere shortening in response to life stress. *Proceedings of the National Academy of Sciences of the United States of America, 101*(49), 17312–17315.

Eriksson, P. S., Perfilieva, E., Björk-Eriksson, T., Alborn, A. M., Nordborg, C., Peterson, D. A., et al. (1998). Neurogenesis in the adult human hippocampus. *Nature Medicine, 4,* 1313–1317.

Erickson, K. I., Voss, M. W., Prakash, R. S., Basak, C., Szabo, A., Chaddock, L., et al. (2011). Exercise training increases size of hippocampus and improves memory. *Proceedings of the National Academy of Sciences of the United States of America, 108*(7), 3017–3022.

Esquith, R. (2007). *Teach like your hair's on fire: The methods and madness inside room.* New York: Penguin Books.

Evans, G. W. (2003). A multimethodological analysis of cumulative risk and allostatic load among rural children. *Developmental Psychology, 39*(5), 924–933.

Evans, G. W. (2004). The environment of childhood poverty. *American Psychologist, 59*(2), 77–92.

Evans, G. W., & English, K. (2002). The environment of poverty: Multiple stressor exposure, psychophysiological stress, and socioemotional adjustment. *Child Development, 73*(4), 1238–1248.

Evans, G. W., & Kantrowitz, E. (2002). Socioeconomic status and health: The potential role of environmental risk exposure. *Annual Review of Public Health, 23*, 303–331.

Evans, G. W., & Kim, P. (2012). Childhood poverty and young adults' allostatic load: the mediating role of childhood cumulative risk exposure. *Psychological Science*, 23, 979–983.

Evans G. W., Fuller-Rowell, T. E. (2013). Childhood poverty, chronic stress, and young adult working memory: the protective role of self-regulatory capacity. *Developmental Science, 16*, 688–696.

Evans, G. W., & Schamberg, M. A. (2009). Childhood poverty, chronic stress, and adult working memory. *Proceedings of the National Academy of Sciences of the United States of America, 106*(16), 6545–6549.

Farah, M. J., Shera, D. M., Savage, J. H., Betancourt, L., Giannetta, J. M., Brodsky, N. L., et al. (2006). Childhood poverty: Specific associations with neurocognitive development. *Brain Research, 1110*(1), 166–174.

Farr, S. (2010). *Teaching as leadership: The highly effective teacher's guide to closing the achievement gap*. San Francisco: Jossey-Bass.

Ferguson, R. F. (1998). Can schools narrow the black-white test score gap? In C. Jencks & M. Phillips (Eds.), *The black-white test score gap* (pp. 318–374). Washington, DC: Brookings Institution Press.

Fernald, A., Marchman, V. A., & Weisleder, A. (2013). SES differences in language processing skill and vocabulary are evident at 18 months. *Developmental Science, 16*(2), 234–248.

Flores, D., Lemons, A., & McTernan, H. (2011). *The correlation between student growth mindset and conceptual development in physics*. Accessed at http://modeling.asu.edu /modeling/Mindset&Physics-McT,L,F.pdf on January 6, 2016.

Forgeard, M., Winner, E., Norton, A., & Schlaug, G. (2008). Practicing a musical instrument in childhood is associated with enhanced verbal ability and nonverbal reasoning. *PloS One, 3*(10), e3566.

Fredrickson, B. L., & Branigan, C. (2005). Positive emotions broaden the scope of attention and thought-action repertoires. *Cognition and Emotion, 19*(3), 313–332.

Fredrickson, B. L., Grewen, K. M., Coffey, K. A., Algoe, S. B., Firestine, A. M., Arevalo, J. M., et al. (2013). A functional genomic perspective on human well-being. *Proceedings of the National Academy of Sciences of the United States of America, 110*(33), 13684–13689.

Fredrickson, B. L., & Losada, M. F. (2005). Positive affect and the complex dynamics of human flourishing. *American Psychologist, 60*(7), 678–686.

Fredrickson, B. L., Tugade, M. M., Waugh, C. E., & Larkin, G. R. (2003). What good are positive emotions in crises?: A prospective study of resilience and emotions following the terrorist attacks on the United States on September 11th, 2001. *Journal of Personality and Social Psychology, 84*(2), 365–376.

Froh, J. J., Sefick, W. J., & Emmons, R. A. (2008). Counting blessings in early adolescents: An experimental study of gratitude and subjective well-being. *Journal of School Psychology*, *46*(2), 213–233.

Galatzer-Levy, R. M., & Cohler, B. J. (1993). *The essential other: A developmental psychology of the self*. New York: Basic Books.

Gámez, P. B., & Lesaux, N. K. (2015). Early-adolescents' reading comprehension and the stability of the middle school classroom-language environment. *Developmental Psychology*, *51*(4), 447–458.

Garner, R. (1990). When children and adults do not use learning strategies: Toward a theory of settings. *Review of Educational Research*, *60*(4), 517–529.

Gazzaniga, M. S. (1998). *The mind's past*. Los Angeles: University of California Press.

Ginsborg, J. (2006). The effects of socioeconomic status on children's language acquisition and use. In J. Clegg & J. Ginsborg (Eds.), *Language and social disadvantage: Theory Into practice* (pp. 9–27). San Francisco: Wiley.

Godfrey, K. M., Costello, P. M., & Lillycrop, K. A. (2015). The developmental environment, epigenetic biomarkers and long-term health. *Journal of Developmental Origins of Health and Disease*, *5*, 399–406.

Goldin, A. P., Hermida, M. J., Shalom, D. E., Elias Costa, M., Lopez-Rosenfeld, M., Segretin, M. S, et al. (2014). Far transfer to language and math of a short software-based gaming intervention. *Proceedings of the National Academy of Sciences of the United States of America*, *111*, 6443–6448.

Goldin, P. R., McRae, K., Ramel, W., & Gross, J. J. (2008). The neural bases of emotion regulation: Reappraisal and suppression of negative emotion. *Biological Psychiatry*, *63*(6), 577–586.

Gottfried, A. W., Gottfried, A. E., Bathurst, K., Guerin, D.W., & Parramore, M. M. (2003). Socioeconomic status in children's development and family environment: Infancy through adolescence. In M. H. Bornstein & R. H. Bradley (Eds.), *Socioeconomic status, parenting, and child development* (pp. 189–207). Mahwah, NJ: Erlbaum Associates.

Governing. (2015). *Bankrupt cities, municipalities list and map*. Accessed at www.governing.com/gov-data/municipal-cities-counties-bankruptcies-and-defaults.html on January 14, 2016.

Grissom, J. B. (2005). Physical fitness and academic achievement. *Journal of Exercise Physiology*, *8*(1), 11–25.

Hackman, D. A., & Farah, M. J. (2009). Socioeconomic status and the developing brain. *Trends in Cognitive Sciences*, *13*(2), 65–73.

Hafen, C. A., Allen, J. P., Mikami, A. Y., Gregory, A., Hamre, B., & Pianta, R. C. (2012). The pivotal role of adolescent autonomy in secondary school classrooms. *Journal of Youth and Adolescence*, *41*(3), 245–255.

Hammack, P. L., & Toolis, E. (2014). Narrative and the social construction of adulthood. *New Directions for Child and Adolescent Development*, *2014*(145), 43–56.

Harrell, E., Langton, L., Berzofsky, M., Couzens, L., & Smiley-McDonald, H. (2014). *Household poverty and nonfatal violent victimization, 2008–2012.* Washington, DC: U.S. Department of Justice, Office of Justice Programs, Bureau of Justice Statistics.

Hart, B., & Risley, T. R. (1995). *Meaningful differences in the everyday experience of young American children.* Baltimore: Brookes.

Hart, B., & Risley, T. R. (2003). The early catastrophe: The 30 million word gap by age 3. *American Educator, 27*, 4–9.

Hattie, J. (2009). *Visible learning: A synthesis of over 800 meta-analyses relating to achievement.* New York: Routledge.

Hattie, J., Biggs, J., & Purdie, N. (1996). Effects of learning skills interventions on student learning: A meta-analysis. *Review of Educational Research, 66*(2), 99–136.

Hawn, G. (2011). *10 mindful minutes: Giving our children—and ourselves—the social and emotional skills to reduce stress and anxiety for healthier, happier lives.* New York: Penguin.

Headey, B., Muffels, R., & Wagner, G. G. (2010). Long-running German panel survey shows that personal and economic choices, not just genes, matter for happiness. *Proceedings of the National Academy of Sciences of the United States of America, 107*(42), 17922–17926.

Heller, S., Pollack, H. A., Ander, R., & Ludwig, J. (2013). *Preventing youth violence and dropout: A randomized field experiment* (Working Paper No. 19014). Cambridge, MA: National Bureau of Economic Research. Accessed at www.nber.org/papers/w19014 on January 14, 2016.

Himmelstein, M. S., Young, D. M., Sanchez, D. T., & Jackson, J. S. (2015). Vigilance in the discrimination-stress model for Black Americans. *Psychology and Health, 30*(3), 253–267.

Ho, Y.-C., Cheung, M.-C., & Chan, A. S. (2003). Music training improves verbal but not visual memory: Cross-sectional and longitudinal explorations in children. *Neuropsychology, 17*(3), 439–450.

Holmes, J., Gathercole, S. E., Place, M., Dunning, D. L., Hilton, K. A., & Elliott, J. G. (2010). Working memory deficits can be overcome: Impacts of training and medication on working memory in children with ADHD. *Applied Cognitive Psychology, 24*(6), 827–836.

Honora, D. T. (2002). The relationship of gender and achievement to future outlook among African American adolescents. *Adolescence, 37*(146), 301–316.

Hoy, W. K., Tarter, C. J., & Hoy, A. W. (2006). Academic optimism of schools: A force for student achievement. *American Educational Research Journal, 43*(3), 425–446.

Hughes, M. G., Day, E. A., Wang, X., Schuelke, M. J., Arsenault, M. L., Harkrider, L. N., et al. (2013). Learner-controlled practice difficulty in the training of a complex task: Cognitive and motivational mechanisms. *Journal of Applied Psychology, 98*(1), 80–98.

Hurlemann, R., Hawellek, B., Matusch, A., Kolsch, H., Wollersen, H., Madea, B., et al. (2005). Noradrenergic modulation of emotion-induced forgetting and remembering. *Journal of Neuroscience, 25*(27), 6343–6349.

Hyerle, D. (1996). *Visual tools for constructing knowledge.* Alexandria, VA: Association for Supervision and Curriculum Development.

Illinois Public Health Institute. (2013). *Enhancing P.E. in Illinois: Naperville Central High School.* Accessed at http://iphionline.org/pdf/P.E._Case_Study_Naperville.pdf on January 14, 2016.

Irish, J. (2012). *Crush Lusher: Investing students in something bigger than themselves.* Accessed at http://tntp.org/assets/documents/TNTP_FishmanPrizeSeries_2012.pdf on October 22, 2015.

Isen, A. M., Daubman, K. A., & Nowicki, G. P. (1987). Positive affect facilitates creative problem solving. *Journal of Personality and Social Psychology, 52*(6), 1122–1131.

Jensen, E. (n.d.). *The "Bobby McFerrin effect" on your brain.* Accessed at www.jensenlearning.com/news/the-bobby-mcferrin-effect-on-your-brain/bra on April 15, 2016.

Jensen, E. (2014). *A descriptive study of differences between teachers at high and low performing Title I elementary schools* (UMI No. 3616282). Santa Barbara, CA: Fielding Graduate University.

Jerald, C. D. (2001). *Dispelling the myth revisited: Preliminary findings from a nationwide analysis of "high-flying" schools.* Washington, DC: Education Trust.

Johnson, S. M. (2010). How best to add value?: Strike a balance between the individual and the organization in school reform. *Voices in Urban Education, 27,* 7–15.

Kahneman, D. (2013). *Thinking, fast and slow.* New York: Farrar, Straus and Giroux.

Kim, P., Evans, G. W., Angstadt, M., Ho, S. S., Sripada, C. S., Swain, J. E., et al. (2013). Effects of childhood poverty and chronic stress on emotion regulatory brain function in adulthood. *Proceedings of the National Academy of Sciences of the United States of America, 110*(46), 18442–18447.

Kim, P., Neuendorf, C., Bianco, H., & Evans, G. W. (2015). Exposure to childhood poverty and mental health symptomatology in adolescence: A role of coping strategies. *Stress and Health.* Accessed at http://onlinelibrary.wiley.com/doi/10.1002/smi.2646/abstract on May 18, 2016.

Kirschner, P. A., Sweller, J., & Clark, R. E. (2006). Why minimal guidance during instruction does not work: An analysis of the failure of constructivist, discovery, problem-based, experiential, and inquiry-based teaching. *Educational Psychologist, 41*(2), 75–86.

Klanker, M., Feenstra, M., & Denys, D. (2013). Dopaminergic control of cognitive flexibility in humans and animals. *Frontiers in Neuroscience, 7*(201).

Knecht, S., Breitenstein, C., Bushuven, S., Wailke, S., Kamping, S., Flöel, A., et al. (2004). Levodopa: Faster and better word learning in normal humans. *Annals of Neurology, 56*(1), 20–26.

Krashen, S. (2002). *Poverty has a powerful impact on educational attainment, or, don't trust Ed Trust.* Chicago: Substance.

Kraus, M. W., Piff, P. K., & Keltner, D. (2009). Social class, sense of control, and social explanation. *Journal of Personality and Social Psychology, 97*(6), 992–1004.

Layous, K., & Lyubomirsky, S. (2014). The how, why, what, when, and who of happiness: Mechanisms underlying the success of positive activity interventions. In J. Gruber & J. T. Moskowitz (Eds.), *Positive emotion: Integrating the light sides and dark sides* (pp. 473-495). New York: Oxford University Press.

Layous, K., Nelson, S. K., Oberle, E., Schonert-Reichl, K. A., & Lyubomirsky, S. (2012). Kindness counts: Prompting prosocial behavior in preadolescents boosts peer acceptance and well-being. *PLOS ONE, 7*(12).

Lewis, G. J., Kanai, R., Rees, G., & Bates, T. C. (2014). Neural correlates of the "good life": Eudaimonic well-being is associated with insular cortex volume. *Social Cognitive and Affective Neuroscience, 9*(5), 615–618.

Lewitus, G. M., & Schwartz, M. (2009). Behavioral immunization: Immunity to self-antigens contributes to psychological stress resilience. *Molecular Psychiatry, 14*, 532–536.

Lieberman, M. D., Eisenberger, N. I., Crockett, M. J., Tom, S. M., Pfeifer, J. H., & Way, B. M. (2007). Putting feelings into words: Affect labeling disrupts amygdala activity in response to affective stimuli. *Psychological Science, 18*(5), 421–428.

Liu, Y., & Wang, Z. (2014). Positive affect and cognitive control: Approach-motivation intensity influences the balance between cognitive flexibility and stability. *Psychological Science, 25*(5), 1116–1123.

London, R. A., & Castrechini, S. (2011). A longitudinal examination of the link between youth physical fitness and academic achievement. *Journal of School Health, 81*(7), 400–408.

Lyubomirsky, S., Sousa, L., & Dickerhoof, R. (2006). The costs and benefits of writing, talking, and thinking about life's triumphs and defeats. *Journal of Personality and Social Psychology, 90*(4), 692–708.

Lyubomirsky, S., Dickerhoof, R., Boehm, J. K, Sheldon, K. M. (2011). Becoming happier takes both a will and a proper way: an experimental longitudinal intervention to boost well-being. *Emotion, 11*(2), 391–402.

Mackey, A. P., Whitaker, K. J., & Bunge, S. A. (2012). Experience-dependent plasticity in white matter microstructure: Reasoning training alters structural connectivity. *Frontiers in Neuroanatomy, 6*(32), 1–9.

Maier, S. F., & Watkins, L. R. (2005). Stressor controllability and learned helplessness: the roles of the dorsal raphe nucleus, serotonin, and corticotropin-releasing factor. *Neuroscience & Biobehavioral Reviews, 29*, 829–841

Marin-Burgin, A., & Schinder, A. F. (2012). Requirement of adult-born neurons for hippocampus-dependent learning. *Behavioural Brain Research, 227*(2), 391–399.

Marzano, R. J. (1998). *A theory-based meta-analysis of research on instruction.* Aurora, CO: McREL. Accessed at www.peecworks.org/peec/peec_research/I01795EFA.2/Marzano%20Instruction%20Meta_An.pdf on January 6, 2016.

Marzano, R. J. (2001). *Classroom instruction that works: Research-based strategies for increasing student achievement.* Alexandria, VA: Association for Supervision and Curriculum Development.

Marzano, R. J., & Simms, J. A. (2013). *Vocabulary for the Common Core*. Bloomington, IN: Marzano Research.

Marzano, R. J., & Simms, J. A. (2014). *Questioning sequences in the classroom*. Bloomington, IN: Marzano Research.

Maslow, A. H. (1943). A theory of human motivation. *Psychological Review, 50*, 370–396.

Mayer, R. E. (1989). Models for understanding. *Review of Educational Research, 59*(1), 43–64.

Mazziotta, J. C., Woods, R., Iacoboni, M., Sicotte, N., Yaden, K., Tran, M., et al. (2009). The myth of the normal, average human brain—the ICBM experience: (1) Subject screening and eligibility. *Neuroimage, 44*(3), 914–922.

McEwen, B. S. (2002). *The end of stress as we know it*. New York: Dana Press.

McGaugh, J. L. (2013). Making lasting memories: Remembering the significant. *Proceedings of the National Academy of Sciences of the United States of America, 110*(2), 10402–10407.

McTighe, J., & Wiggins, G. (2013). *Essential questions: Opening doors to student understanding*. Alexandria, VA: Association for Supervision and Curriculum Development.

Mehta, J., & Fine, S. (2012). Teaching differently . . . learning deeply. *Phi Delta Kappan, 94*(2), 31–35.

Melby-Lervåg, M., & Hulme, C. (2013). Is working memory training effective?: A meta-analytic review. *Developmental Psychology, 49*(2), 270–291.

Meneses, A., & Liy-Salmeron, G. (2012). Serotonin and emotion, learning and memory. *Reviews in the Neurosciences, 23*(5–6), 543–553.

Milad, M. R., Wright, C. I., Orr, S. P., Pitman, R. K., Quirk, G. J., & Rauch, S. L. (2007). Recall of fear extinction in humans activates the ventromedial prefrontal cortex and hippocampus in concert. *Biological Psychiatry, 62*(5), 446–454.

Miller, G. (1956). Chunks: The magical number seven, plus or minus two: Some limits on our capacity for processing information. *The Psychological Review, 63*, 81–97.

Miller, C. A., & Sweatt, J. D. (2007). Covalent modification of DNA regulates memory formation. *Neuron, 53*(6), 857–869.

Miller, J. C., & Krizan, Z. (2016). Walking facilitates positive affect (even when expecting the opposite). *Emotion*.

Miller-Lewis, L. R., Sawyer, A. C., Searle, A. K., Mittinty, M. N., Sawyer, M. G., & Lynch, J. W. (2014). Student-teacher relationship trajectories and mental health problems in young children. *BMC Psychology, 12*, 27.

Morgan, P. L., Farkas, G., Hillemeier, M. M., & Maczuga, S. (2009). Risk factors for learning-related behavior problems at 24 months of age: Population-based estimates. *Journal of Abnormal Child Psychology, 37*(3), 401–413.

Muncer, S. J., & Knight, D. (2011). The syllable effect in anagram solution: unrecognized evidence from past studies. *Journal of Psycholinguistic Research, 40*, 111–118.

Mueller, C. M., & Dweck, C. S. (1998). Praise for intelligence can undermine children's motivation and performance. *Journal of Personality and Social Psychology, 75*(1), 33–52.

Murty, V. P., DuBrow, S., & Davachi, L. (2015). The simple act of choosing influences declarative memory. *Journal of Neuroscience, 35*(16), 6255–6264.

Nagel, D. (2006). *Music in education: Study finds link with attendance and graduation rates.* Accessed at https://thejournal.com/articles/2006/11/06/music-in-education-study-finds -link-with-attendance-and-graduation-rates.aspx on July 5, 2016.

National Governors Association Center for Best Practices & Council of Chief State School Officers. (2010). *Common Core State Standards for English language arts and literacy in history/social studies, science, and technical subjects.* Washington, DC: Authors. Accessed at www.corestandards.org/assets/CCSSI_ELA%20Standards.pdf on February 25, 2016.

Nelson, P. M., Demers, J. A., & Christ, T. J. (2014). The responsive environmental assessment for classroom teaching (REACT): The dimensionality of student perceptions of the instructional environment. *School Psychology Quarterly, 29,*182–197.

Nicholls, J. G., & Miller, A. T. (1984). Reasoning about the ability of self and others: A developmental study. *Child Development, 55,* 1990–1999.

The New Teacher Project. (2013). *Josalyn Tresvant.* Accessed at http://tntp.org/fishman-prize/winners/fishman-prize-2013/josalyn-tresvant on May 31, 2016.

Nesbitt, R. E. (2009). *Intelligence and how to get it: Why schools and cultures count.* New York: Norton.

NGSS Lead States. (2013). *Next Generation Science Standards: For states, by states.* Washington, DC: The National Academies Press.

Noble, K. G., Norman, M. F., & Farah, M. J. (2005). Neurocognitive correlates of socioeconomic status in kindergarten children. *Developmental Science, 8*(1), 74–87.

Noble, K. G., Tottenham, N., & Casey, B. J. (2005). Neuroscience perspectives on disparities in school readiness and cognitive achievement. *Future of Children, 15*(1), 71–89.

NPR, Robert Wood Johnson Foundation, & Harvard School of Public Health. (2013). *Education and health in schools: A survey of parents. Summary.* Accessed at www.rwjf .org/content/dam/farm/reports/surveys_and_polls/2013/rwjf407960 on June 2, 2016.

Oberle, E., Schonert-Reichl, K. A., & Thomson, K. C. (2010). Understanding the link between social and emotional well-being and peer relations in early adolescence: Gender-specific predictors of peer acceptance. *Journal of Youth and Adolescence, 39*(11), 1330–1342.

Ohira, K., Takeuchi, R., Shoji, H., & Miyakawa, T. (2013). Fluoxetine-induced cortical adult neurogenesis. *Neuropsychopharmacology, 38*(6), 909–920.

O'Keefe, P. A., & Linnenbrink-Garcia, L. (2014). The role of interest in optimizing performance and self-regulation. *Journal of Experimental Social Psychology, 53,* 70–78.

Online College. (2012, June 27). *12 reasons community service should be required in schools.* Accessed at www.onlinecollege.org/2012/06/27/12-reasons-community-service-should-be-required-schools on May 27, 2016.

Olejnik, S., & Algina, J. (2000). Measures of effect size for comparative studies: Applications, interpretations, and limitations. *Contemporary Educational Psychology, 25*(3), 241–286.

O'Rourke, N., Haimovitz, K., Ballweber, C., Dweck, C. S., & Popović, Z. (2014). *Brain points: A growth mindset incentive structure boosts persistence in an educational game.* Proceedings of the ACM Conference on Human Factors in Computing Systems (CHI 2014), Toronto.

Otake, K., Shimai, S., Tanaka-Matsumi, J., Otsui, K., & Fredrickson, B. L. (2006). Happy people become happier through kindness: A counting kindnesses intervention. *Journal of Happiness Studies, 7*(3), 361–375.

Ouweneel, E., Le Blanc, P. M., & Schaufeli, W. B. (2014). On being grateful and kind: Results of two randomized controlled trials on study-related emotions and academic engagement. *Journal of Health Psychology, 148*(1), 37–60.

Palardy, G. J., & Rumberger, R. W. (2008). Teacher effectiveness in first grade: The importance of background qualifications, attitudes, and instructional practices for student learning. *Educational Evaluation and Policy Analysis, 30*(2), 111–140.

Parrett, W. H., & Budge, K. M. (2012). *Turning high-poverty schools into high-performing schools.* Alexandria, VA: Association for Supervision and Curriculum Development.

Parsad, B., & Spiegelman, M. (2012). *Arts education in public elementary and secondary schools: 1999–2000 and 2009–2010.* Accessed http://nces.ed.gov/pubs2012/2012014rev.pdf on June 2, 2016.

Passolunghi, M. C., Vercelloni, B., & Schadee, H. (2007). The precursors of mathematics learning: Working memory, phonological ability and numerical competence. *Cognitive Development, 22*(2), 165–184.

Pereira, A. C., Huddleston, D. E., Brickman, A. M., Sosunov, A. A., Hen, R., McKhann, G. M., et al. (2007). An in vivo correlate of exercise-induced neurogenesis in the adult dentate gyrus. *Proceedings of the National Academy of Sciences of the United States of America, 104*(13), 5638–5643.

Petty, G. (2009). *Evidence-based teaching: A practical approach.* Cheltenham, United Kingdom: Nelson Thornes.

Ping, R., & Goldin-Meadow, S. (2010). Gesturing saves cognitive resources when talking about nonpresent objects. *Cognitive Science, 34*, 602–619.

Pew Research Center. (2016). *America's shrinking middle class: A close look at changes within metropolitan areas.* Accessed at www.pewsocialtrends.org/2016/05/11/americas-shrinking-middle-class-a-close-look-at-changes-within-metropolitan-areas on May 18, 2016.

Plomin, R., Haworth, C. M., & Davis, O. S. (2009). Common disorders are quantitative traits. *Nature Reviews Genetics, 10*(12), 872–878.

Pratt, L. A., & Brody, D. J. (2014). *NCHS data brief: Depression in the U.S. household population, 2009–2012* (No. 172). Hyattsville, MD: National Center for Health Statistics.

Priest, N., Paradies, Y., Trenerry, B., Truong, M., Karlsen, S., & Kelly, Y. (2013). A systematic review of studies examining the relationship between reported racism and health and wellbeing for children and young people. *Social Science and Medicine, 95*, 115–127.

Rank, M. R., & Hirschl, T. A. (2015). The likelihood of experiencing relative poverty over the life course. *PLoS ONE, 10*(7), e0133513.

Ratey, J. J. (2008). *Spark: The revolutionary new science of exercise and the brain*. New York: Little, Brown.

Rattan, A., Savani, K., Chugh, D., & Dweck, C. S. (2015). Leveraging mindsets to promote academic achievement: policy recommendations. *Perspective Psychology Science, 10*, 721–726.

Rauner, R. R., Walters, R. W., Avery, M., & Wanser, T. J. (2013) Evidence that aerobic fitness is more salient than weight status in predicting standardized math and reading outcomes in fourth- through eighth-grade students. *Journal of Pediatrics, 163*(2), 344–348.

Raver, C. C., Blair, C., & Willoughby, M. (2013). Poverty as a predictor of 4-year-olds' executive function: New perspectives on models of differential susceptibility. *Developmental Psychology, 49*(2), 292–304.

Reeves, L. M., & Weisberg, R. W. (1994). The role of content and abstract information in analogical transfer. *Psychological Bulletin, 115*(3), 381–400.

Ritchhart, R., Church, M., & Morrison, K. (2011). *Making thinking visible: How to promote engagement, understanding, and independence for all learners*. San Francisco: Jossey-Bass.

Robertson-Kraft, C., & Duckworth, A. L. (2014). True grit: Trait-level perseverance and passion for long-term goals predicts effectiveness and retention among novice teachers. *Teachers College Record, 116*(3), 1–27.

Roediger, H. L., III, Agarwal, P. K., McDaniel, M. A., & McDermott, K. B. (2011). Test-enhanced learning in the classroom: Long-term improvements from quizzing. *Journal of Experimental Psychology: Applied, 17*(4), 382–395.

Rowe, G., Hirsh, J. B., & Anderson, A. K. (2007). Positive affect increases the breadth of attentional selection. *Proceedings of the National Academy of Sciences of the United States of America, 104*(1), 383–388.

Ruhl, K. L., Hughes, C. A., & Schloss, P. J. (1987). Using the pause procedure to enhance lecture recall. *Teacher Education and Special Education, 10*, 14–18.

Russell, I. J., Hendricson, W. D., & Herbert, R. J. (1984). Effects of lecture information density on medical student achievement. *Journal of Medical Education, 59*(11), 881–889.

Russo, N. M., Hornickel, H., Nicol, T., Zecker, S., & Kraus, N. (2010). Biological changes in auditory function following training in children with autism spectrum disorders. *Behavioral and Brain Functions, 6*(60), 1–8.

Ryff, C. D. (2014). Self-realization and meaning making in the face of adversity: A eudaimonic approach to human resilience. *South African Journal of Psychology, 24*, 1–12.

Sartori, G., Lombardi, L., & Mattiuzzi, L. (2005). Semantic relevance best predicts normal and abnormal name retrieval. *Neuropsychologia, 43*(5), 754–770.

Schaefer, S., Lovden, M., Wieckhorst, B., & Lindenberger, U. (2010). Cognitive performance is improved while walking: Differences in cognitive-sensorimotor couplings between children and young adults. *European Journal of Developmental Psychology, 7*, 371–389

Scheffer, B. K., & Rubenfeld, M. G. (2001). Critical thinking: What is it and how do we teach it? In J. M. Dochterman & H. K. Grace (Eds.), *Current issues in nursing* (6th ed.; pp. 352–359). St. Louis, MO: Mosby.

Schellenberg, E. G. (2004). Music lessons enhance IQ. *Psychological Science, 15*(8), 511–514.

Schoenthaler, S. J., Bier, I. D., Young, K., Nichols, D., & Jansenns, S. (2000). The effect of vitamin-mineral supplementation on the intelligence of American schoolchildren: A randomized, double-blind placebo-controlled trial. *Journal of Alternative and Complementary Medicine, 6*(1), 19–29.

Scruggs, T. E., Mastropieri, M. A., Berkeley, S., & Graetz, J. E. (2010). Do special education interventions improve learning of secondary content?: A meta-analysis. *Remedial and Special Education, 31*(6), 437–449.

Segretin, M. S., Lipina, S. J., Hermida, M. J., Sheffield, T. D., Nelson, J. M., Espy, K. A., et al. (2014). Predictors of cognitive enhancement after training in preschoolers from diverse socioeconomic backgrounds. *Frontiers in Psychology, 5*(205).

Seligman, M. E. P. (2006). *Learned optimism: How to change your mind and your life.* New York: Vintage.

Serrano, M. A., Moya-Albiol, L., & Salvador, A. (2014). Endocrine and mood responses to two working days in female teachers. *Spanish Journal of Psychology, 17*(e25), 1–11.

Sesma, H. W., Mahone, E. M., Levine, T., Eason, S. H., & Cutting, L. E. (2009). The contribution of executive skills to reading comprehension. *Child Neuropsychology, 15*(3), 232–246.

ShadowStats.com. (2016). *Alternate inflation charts.* Accessed at www.shadowstats.com /alternate_data/inflation-charts on January 6, 2016.

Shah, A. K., Mullainathan, S., & Shafir, E. (2014). Some consequences of having too little. *Science, 338,* 682–685.

Sharot, T., Shiner, T., Brown, A. C., Fan, J., & Dolan, R. J. (2009). Dopamine enhances expectation of pleasure in humans. *Current Biology, 19*(24), 2077–2080.

Sheldon, K. M., & Lyubomirsky, S. (2006). How to increase and sustain positive emotion: The effects of expressing gratitude and visualizing best possible selves. *The Journal of Positive Psychology, 1,* 73–82.

Shellshear, L., MacDonald, A. D., Mahoney, J., Finch, E., McMahon, K., Silburn, P., et al. (2015). Levodopa enhances explicit new-word learning in healthy adults: A preliminary study. *Human Psychopharmacology: Clinical and Experimental, 30*(5), 341–349.

Shinaver C. S., III, Entwistle, P. C., & Söderqvist S. (2014). *Cogmed WM training: Reviewing the reviews. Applied Neuropsychological Child, 3,* 163–172.

Shors, T. J., Olson, R. L., Bates, M. E., Selby, E. A., & Alderman, B. L. (2014). Mental and physical (MAP) training: A neurogenesis-inspired intervention that enhances health in humans. *Neurobiology of Learning and Memory, 115,* 3–9.

Siegler, R. S., & Alibali, M. W. (2005). *Children's thinking* (4th ed.). Upper Saddle River, NJ: Pearson.

Singh, M., & Singh, G. (2005). Assessment of mental health status of middle-aged female school teachers of Varanasi city. *Internet Journal of Health, 5*(1), 1–10.

Skeels, H. M. (1966). Adult status of children with contrasting early experience: a follow-up study. *Monographs of the Society for Research in Child Development, 31*, 1–65

Skoe, E., & Kraus, N. (2012). A little goes a long way: How the adult brain is shaped by musical training in childhood. *The Journal of Neuroscience, 3*(34), 11507–11510.

Social Security Online. (2016). *Wage statistics for 2014*. Accessed at www.ssa.gov/cgi-bin/netcomp.cgi?year=2014 on January 6, 2016.

Söderqvist, S., & Nutley, S. B. (2015). Working memory training is associated with long term attainments in math and reading. *Frontiers in Psychology, 10*, 1711.

Soloveichik, S. (1979, May). Odd way to teach, but it works. *Soviet Life Magazine, 5*, 18–22.

Southgate, D. E., & Roscigno, V. J. (2009). The impact of music on childhood and adolescent achievement. *Social Science Quarterly, 90*(1), 4–21.

Spilt, J. L., Koomen, H. M., & Harrison, L. J. (2015). Language development in the early school years: The importance of close relationships with teachers. *Developmental Psychology, 51*(2), 185–196.

Sripada, R. K., Swain, J. E., Evans, G. W., Welsh, R. C., & Liberzon, I. (2014). Childhood poverty and stress reactivity are associated with aberrant functional connectivity in default mode network. *Neuropsychopharmacology, 39*(9), 2244–2251.

Standley, J. M. (2008). Does music instruction help children learn to read? Evidence of a meta-analysis. *Update: Applications of Research in Music Education, 27*, 17–32.

Steptoe, A., Wardle, J., & Marmot, M. (2005). Positive affect and health-related neuroendocrine, cardiovascular, and inflammatory processes. *Proceedings of the National Academy of Sciences of the United States of America, 102*(18), 6508–6512.

Swanson, C. B. (2009). *Cities in crisis 2009: Closing the graduation gap—Educational and economic conditions in America's largest cities*. Bethesda, MD: Editorial Projects in Education. Accessed at www.edweek.org/media/cities_in_crisis_2009.pdf on January 13, 2016.

Sweller, J., van Merrienboer, J. J. G., & Paas, F. G. W. C. (1998). Cognitive architecture and instructional design. *Educational Psychology Review, 10*(3), 251–296.

Suitts, S. (2015). *A new majority research bulletin: Low income students now a majority in the nation's public schools*. Atlanta, GA: Southern Education Foundation. Accessed at www.southerneducation.org/Our-Strategies/Research-and-Publications/New-Majority-Diverse-Majority-Report-Series/A-New-Majority-2015-Update-Low-Income-Students-Now.aspx on January 6, 2016.

Telzer, E. H., Fuligni, A. J., Lieberman, M. D., & Galván, A. (2014). Neural sensitivity to eudaimonic and hedonic rewards differentially predict adolescent depressive symptoms over time. *Proceedings of the National Academy of Sciences of the United States of America, 111*(18), 6600–6605.

Toga, A. (2005, October 15). Keynote address at the Learning Brain EXPO in Newport Beach, CA.

Tomlinson, C. A. (2014). *The differentiated classroom: Responding to the needs of all learners* (2nd ed.). Alexandria, VA: Association for Supervision and Curriculum Development.

Tucker-Drob, E. M., Rhemtulla, M., Harden, K. P., Turkheimer, E., & Fask, D. (2011). Emergence of a Gene X socioeconomic status interaction on infant mental ability between 10 months and 2 years. *Psychological Science, 22*, 125–133.

Ullman, S. E., Townsend, S., Filipas, H. H., & Starzynski, L. L. (2007). Structural models of the relations of assault severity, social support, avoidance coping, self-blame, and PTSD among sexual assault survivors. *Psychology of Women Quarterly, 31*(1), 23–37.

Urban Prep Academies. (2016). *Urban Prep announces 100% of seniors admitted to college and launch of "10andchange" campaign to refocus the narrative of black boys/young men on positive stories.* Accessed at www.prnewswire.com/news-releases/urban-prep-announces-100-of-seniors-admitted-to-college-and-launch-of-10andchange-campaign-to-refocus-the-narrative-of-black-boysyoung-men-on-positive-stories-300237717.html on June 2, 2016.

U.S. Census Bureau. (n.d.). *Survey of income and program participation.* Accessed at www.census.gov/programs-surveys/sipp.html on January 6, 2016.

U.S. Census Bureau. (2011). *More young adults are living in their parents' home, Census Bureau reports* [Press release]. Accessed at www.census.gov/newsroom/releases/archives/families_households/cb11-183.html on January 6, 2016.

U.S. Department of Agriculture, Food and Nutrition Service. (2016). *Supplemental Nutrition Assistance Program participation and costs.* Accessed at www.fns.usda.gov/sites/default/files/pd/SNAPsummary.pdf January 6, 2016.

U.S. Department of Labor, Bureau of Labor Statistics. (2015). *The employment situation—December 2015* [Press release]. Accessed at www.bls.gov/news.release/pdf/empsit.pdf on January 14, 2016.

U.S. News & World Report. (2016). *High schools: Preuss School UCSD.* Accessed www.usnews.com/education/best-high-schools/california/districts/san-diego-unified-school-district/preuss-school-ucsd-3216 on June 1, 2016.

Vacha-Haase, T., & Thompson, B. (2004). How to estimate and interpret various effect sizes. *Journal of Counseling Psychology, 51*(4), 473–481.

van Gelder, T. (2004). *Using argument mapping to improve critical thinking skills.* Accessed at www.reasoninglab.com/wp-content/uploads/2013/10/TvG-Using-argument-mapping-to-improve-critical-thinking-skills-2015.pdf on May 18, 2016.

van Gelder, T., Bissett, M., & Cumming, G. (2004). Cultivating expertise in informal reasoning. *Canadian Journal of Experimental Psychology, 58*(2), 142–152.

van Holstein, M., Aarts, E., van der Schaaf, M. E., Geurts, D. E., Verkes, R. J., Franke, B., et al. (2011). Human cognitive flexibility depends on dopamine D2 receptor signaling. *Psychopharmacology, 218*(3), 567–578.

van Praag, H., Fleshner, M., Schwartz, M. W., & Mattson, M. P. (2014). Exercise, energy intake, glucose homeostasis, and the brain. *Journal of Neuroscience, 34*(46), 15139–15149.

Vargas Lascano, D. I., Galambos, N. L., Krahn, H. J., & Lachman, M. E. (2015). Growth in perceived control across 25 years from the late teens to midlife: The role of personal and parents' education. *Developmental Psychology, 51*(1), 124–135.

Volkow, N. D., Wang, G. J., Fowler, J. S., Telang, F., Maynard, L., Logan, J., et al. (2004). Evidence that methylphenidate enhances the saliency of a mathematical task by increasing dopamine in the human brain. *American Journal of Psychiatry, 161*(7), 1173–1180.

Voss, J. L., Gonsalves, B. D., Federmeier, K. D., Tranel, D., & Cohen, N. J. (2011). Hippocampal brain-network coordination during volitional exploratory behavior enhances learning. *Nature Neuroscience, 14*(1), 115–120.

Wegner, M., Schüler, J., & Budde, H. (2014). The implicit affiliation motive moderates cortisol responses to acute psychosocial stress in high school students. *Psychoneuroendocrinology, 48*, 162–168.

Willingham, D. T. (2008, Summer). Critical thinking: Why is it so hard to teach? *American Educator, 109*, 21–29.

Winn, W. (2003). Research methods and types of evidence for research in educational technology. *Educational Psychology Review, 15*(4), 367–373.

Winter, B., Breitenstein, C., Mooren, F. C., Voelker, K., Fobker, M., Lechtermann, A., et al. (2007). High impact running improves learning. *Neurobiology of Learning and Memory, 87*(4), 597–609.

World Memory Sports Council. (2015). *World Memory Championships 2015: Names and faces result*. Accessed at www.worldmemorychampionships.com/wp-content /uploads/2015/12/WMC-2015-Full-Scores.pdf on May 14, 2016.

Yamashita, A. (2015). *Mindfulness for beginners: A practical guide to awakening and finding inner peace in your life!* Seattle, WA: CreateSpace.

Yau, S. Y., Li, A., Xu, A., & So, K.-F. (2015). Fat cell-secreted adiponectin mediates physical exercise-induced hippocampal neurogenesis: An alternative anti-depressive treatment? *Neural Regeneration Research, 10*(1), 7–9.

Yehuda, R., Flory, J. D., Southwick, S., & Charney, D. S. (2006). Developing an agenda for translational studies of resilience and vulnerability following trauma exposure. *Annals of the New York Academy of Sciences, 1071*, 379–396.

Zak, P. J. (2015, February). Why inspiring stories make us react: The neuroscience of narrative. *Cerebrum*. Accessed at www.dana.org/Cerebrum/2015/Why_Inspiring_ Stories_Make_Us_React__The_Neuroscience_of_Narrative/ on January 13, 2016.

Zepeda, C. D., Richey, J. E., Ronevich, P., & Nokes-Malach, T. J. (2015). Direct instruction of metacognition benefits adolescent science learning, transfer, and motivation: An in vivo study. *Journal of Educational Psychology, 107*(4), 954–970.

Index

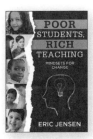

Poor Students, Rich Teaching
Eric Jensen
Discover research-based strategies to ensure all students, regardless of circumstance, are college and career ready. This thorough resource details the necessary but difficult work that teachers must do to establish the foundational changes that positively impact students in poverty.
BKF603

Closing the RTI Gap
Donna Walker Tileston
Get a clear understanding of poverty and culture, and learn how RTI can close achievement gaps related to these issues. Learn how you can achieve successful implementation in your school. Examine common pitfalls to avoid in the process.
BKF330

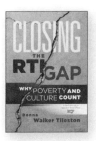

Mind, Brain, & Education
Edited by David A. Sousa
Understanding how the brain learns helps teachers do their jobs more effectively. Primary researchers in the emerging field of educational neuroscience share the latest findings on the learning process and address their implications for educational theory and practice.
BKF358

Building a Culture of Hope
Robert D. Barr and Emily L. Gibson
Discover a blueprint for turning low-performing schools into Cultures of Hope! The authors draw from their own experiences working with high-poverty, high-achieving schools to illustrate how to support students with an approach that considers social as well as emotional factors.
BKF503

Wait! Your professional development journey doesn't have to end with the last pages of this book.

We realize improving student learning doesn't happen overnight. And your school or district shouldn't be left to puzzle out all the details of this process alone.

No matter where you are on the journey, we're committed to helping you get to the next stage.

Take advantage of everything from **custom workshops** to **keynote presentations** and **interactive web and video conferencing**. We can even help you develop an action plan tailored to fit your specific needs.

Let's get the conversation started.

Call 888.763.9045 today.